CHANGUITO

A Master's Approach to Timbales

By Jose Luis Quintana
"Changuito"
written in collaboration with Chuck Silverman

Transcriptions, Text, and Research: Chuck Silverman
Audio Recording and Production: Chuck Silverman
Congas and Clave on CD: Chuck Silverman
Photographs: Chuck Silverman and Susanne Moss
Production Coordinators: Joe Testa and Diane Laucirica
Cover Design: Odalis Soto
Book Design, Typesetting, Music Engraving and Photo Editing: Ed Uribe

© 1998 BELWIN-MILLS PUBLISHING CORP. (ASCAP)
All Rights Assigned to and Controlled by ALFRED MUSIC PUBLISHING, CO., INC.
All Rights Reserved including Public Performance

CW01052363

CHANGUITO

A Master's Approach to Timbales

By Jose Luis Quintana
"Changuito"
written in collaboration with Chuck Silverman

FOREWORD

In July of 1997 I was given the opportunity to spend two weeks in La Habana (Havana), Cuba with the purpose of gathering information for this book. The main source of this information is Jose Luis Quintana, "Changuito." Changuito and I spent many hours together, working on this project. My goal was to capture the magic in his timbale mastery and present it in an educational book/CD package.

With this in mind, I brought all of the technology I could to Cuba. I equipped myself with a portable DAT machine, microphones, powerbook computer, video camera, and plenty of notes and manuscript paper, preparing to capture every performance and musical nuance and bring them to life through this book. It would be these recordings, both audio and visual, that insured all of this important information would be transcribed accurately once back in the States. This information is the foundation upon which this book and CD package are built.

Each day I brought equipment to our "studio," meticulously preparing for the day's work. This was no easy task. Our "studio" was five flights up, with no elevators, and remember, this was July in the Tropics!

I am honored that Changuito asked me to co-author his book. He has been a drumming idol for so many years and working with him is a humbling experience. I want to bring his mastery of the instrument to all those who search for the inspirational and educational material relevant to learning about timbales. To that end, I spent ten days, after all the recordings and work with Changuito was finished, in various schools, libraries, and music institutions, interviewing music professionals, and researching the roots of the instrument. It may have been tedious, but as you read, play, and study from this package, we hope that you agree it was worth the effort.

Chuck Silverman

Changuito and Chuck in La Habana, 1996

TABLE OF CONTENTS AND AUDIO INDEX

ACKNOWLEDGEMENTS

I would like to acknowledge and express my deepest appreciation to Cristóbal Sosa López, for his indispensable efforts in the gathering of information for this project. In addition, I would like to thank the following people and institutions that helped in the research for this project.

Cristóbal Sosa López

Very Special Thanks to:

Sandy Feldstein, Robin Moore, Radames Giro, Amadito Valdés, Elpidio Serra Fundora "Cheverongo," Filiberto Sanchez Aguiar, Jose Manuel Sanchez, Girardo "Piloto" Barreto, Yonder DeJesus Peña Llovet, Raul Pineda Roque, Jimmy Branly, Caribbean Music and Dance Programs, Enrique Pla, Jose Eladio, Biblioteca Naciónal Jose Marti (National Library), Museo Naciónal de la Musica (National Music Museum), Ligia Guzman, Instituto de Historia, Centro Odilio Urfe, Instituto del Literatura y Linguistica de Cuba, Dania Vazquez and Raul Artiles.

Special Thanks to:

Dr. Olavo Alén Rodriguez, Lic. Ana Casanova, Lic. Layda Ferrando, Tamara Sevila, Lic. Liliana Casanella, Centro De Investigación Y Desarrollo De La Musica Cubana (The Center for the Investigation and Development of Cuban Music) "CIDMUC," Ramon Casales, George Casales, Bruce Polin and Descarga, George Rivera, Manny Lopez, Mark Zanger, and everyone who assisted with this project.

A Word About the Recording

Recorded at: Quintana Studios, Reparto Antonio Guiteras, La Habana, Cuba, July 1996
Edited at: Balsam Pillow Music Production, Boca Raton, FL

Disclosure of all of the sounds
i.e.: cars and trucks, car horns, roosters, telephones, people yelling, and so on.

The accompanying CD was recorded in "Quintana Studios," high above the Havana neighborhood of Reparto Antonio Guiteras. "Quintana Studios" is Changuito's home. Imagine the scene in Quintana Studios; mid-July in Havana, no air-conditioning, no fan, no sound-proofing, all this technology, and the master himself recording this book for you!

Throughout the CD you will be entertained by the percussion mastery of Changuito. You will also hear sounds of the neighborhood: car horns, kids playing, roosters and other pets. Rather than attempt to digitally edit out all of these sounds some, such as telephones ringing, have been omitted, many have been left in the recording. The flavor of the CD reflects the music; it reflects life. When you hear these sounds, just picture yourself studying with Changuito (who refused to stop each time a rooster crowed or a truck rolled by!!).

JOSE LUIS QUINTANA~CHANGUITO

Introduction
and Solo

gressed, so did Changuito's style. What started out as just timbales was soon replaced by a full drum set. Changuito's drum set mastery on the song "Guararé," from an early Van Van recording, was a real eye-opener for those of us who had the opportunity to hear it. This was new drumming; cutting edge, hard-hitting and soulful. But the drum set era did not last. The timbales beckoned and Changuito returned. A new style of playing timbales was about to begin. And Changuito would forever change the drumming of the whole world.

Typical patterns, like cáscara, were altered slightly, a note accented or doubled in such a way as to flavor the groove in a new and exciting way. The timbale bells were also subject to change. New patterns were invented, discarded, renewed, reworked, all in the name of groove and swing.

One of the most amazing things, to many drummers and percussionists worldwide, was the new vocabulary of fills and solos which Changuito offered. Chances were taken at almost every opportunity to be outlandish, unpredictable, and still retain the groove and swing. Fills seemed to come out of left field, darting around hair-pin turns, and returning only to fall short or after the downbeat, adding to the tension created by the clave-influenced rhythms. It must have been something to be a musician performing in Los Van Van at this tumultuous time, not knowing where or when one of these fantastic fills would occur. They call him El Misterioso (The Mysterious One). His ideas emanate from some hidden cave of creativity, and boil up to the surface in volcanic eruptions. Without all of these, Los Van Van would have still been great. With the addition of Changuito and his inventive nature, Los Van Van remained at the pinnacle of Cuban popularity for decades.

Jose Luis Quintana, Changuito, drummer and percussionist extraordinaire, has influenced many drummers around the world. As timbalero and drum set artist with the seminal Cuban group, Los Van Van, Changuito helped set the stage for what would be one of the major percussion innovations emanating from Cuba: the rhythm of Songo. This major addition to modern drum set and percussion repertoire has helped to changed the way many drummers play "latin" music.

From the early '70s to the '90s, Changuito forged new percussion ground, propelling Los Van Van to international fame. Los Van Van toured throughout the world, bringing their new swinging grooves to thousands and thousands of dancers, musicians, and new converts to the Afro-Cuban pulse. As the years pro-

Changuito's recorded solos are rare things of beauty. They have influenced generations of Cuban percussionists, in turn influencing us all. You may ask if solos can have such a dramatic effect. My answer is an unqualified yes. Incorporating his trademark unpredictability, flashes of technical genius, and solid Afro-Cuban roots, Changuito's solos are highly prized pieces of art. And, as such, they contain prize nuggets of percussive and musical inspiration for those willing to take the time to absorb and understand the sweat and strain from whence they came.

A relatively new addition to Changuito's percussion arsenal is his extreme independence. Why extreme? To this drummer, Chango's independence at times seems like it is at the apex of its development. One example of this development might be playing the cáscara pattern with the right hand while the left hand solos on the two drums and other bells. This is not just independence, it really is art. It seems that the body has been split in two, that two brains occupy the same skull. The most amazing thing is that each pattern is steeped in feel and musical meaning. Practicing and performing these patterns is a humbling experience.

Above all, Changuito plays from his heart. The man is not going to sit down and write out exercises for you. He doesn't slow his grooves down for you either. "This is not how they sound." "How can I play it this way if I cannot feel it this way." Well, it's a different way of learning. Coming from a country steeped in rhythm, where clave seeps from the soil and is part of the very air, learning can also be different. There are wonderful music schools in Cuba where young musicians can learn and practice their art. Changuito was not allowed to attend. His learning came from the music which surrounded him. A true innovator and master of his craft, Jose Luis Quintana will forever be known as a Master Drummer.

—*Chuck Silverman*

HOW TO PRACTICE THIS BOOK

Practice Rules:
 1. *Practice slowly.*
 2. *Listen to what you play.*
 3. *Watch what you play.*
 4. *Feel for any tension while you are playing.*
 5. *Sing the different rhythms.*

1. Practice Slowly:

Practice slowly and methodically those phrases and exercises which give you the most problem. It is very easy to give up and try to get by these patterns. If you stick with it and really learn the patterns you will find your playing and your confidence improving. In this way, other patterns will become less of a bother, easier to learn, and your playing will get better.

2. Listen:

Listen to what you play. There are many subtle areas in this book: accents and ghosted notes, mouth and body of certain cowbells, sticking patterns which may be unfamiliar to you. (Ghosted notes are notes which are played much more softly than a regular note. A ghosted note will also be notated a bit differently.) Listening to what you are playing helps you to do the most important thing in order to learn: concentrate. Listen to the sound of the hembra (the large timbale), and to the sound of the crack of the macho (the smaller drum). Listen to the difference between the bells and the different sounds each bell has to offer you. Listen to the sound of the cáscara (the sound of the shell of the timbales, as well as a typical pattern). Is it sharp and definite, or is it dull? By listening you are putting more of yourself into the work and you are spending your time wisely.

3. Watch:

Watch what you play. Pay attention to where the stick hits the drum. For the rim shot of the macho, compare your stick position to the pictures at the bottom of page 22. Likewise, when playing cáscara, the position of your stick(s) has a lot to do with the sound you are getting out of the shells and the drums.

4. Feel:

When encountering patterns which require your learning new independent movements, pay attention to how your body feels. Are you relaxed during these patterns and exercises? Are you playing slow enough to where you are performing in a calm manner? Or are you tense? Perhaps performing a bit too fast? By paying attention to signs of tension in your body, you can better tune in to the exercises which may need more work and/or more time. Don't neglect the tension in your shoulders when trying to play mambo bell and clave, nor the stiff feeling in your forearms when practicing the chacha bell pattern. These signs can actually assist you in the learning process!

5. Sing

One other technique which you can use is to sing the lines you are learning. If it is a musical line with two voices (i.e. bell and drum), play one voice and sing the other. This method of learning is another way to internalize the rhythms you are learning.

There are patterns in this book for drummers of all levels. For those of you who find yourself really challenged by some of the patterns which require a high level of independence, remember that these patterns are not meant as exercises. They are real, usable grooves which just happen to be different than what you are used to playing. Your playing will improve as will your feel. Give all of these patterns a chance to enhance your percussion skills.

This book is very special in that it brings to you one of the premier artists in the field of Afro-Cuban music, Jose Luis Quintana, Changuito. It contains very important information and needs to be practiced with special care and attention. Included throughout are tips on how to go about learning and applying these patterns. Most important are some very basic practice concepts.

These five relatively simple rules will help you immensely in the learning and application of the rhythms and ideas found in this book.

The Time Signature used most often in this book: Which time signature to use for the writing of this book, 2/4, 4/4, common time, or 2/2 (cut time)? Music in Cuba is written in all three different time signatures. (Yes, for all of you two-bar phrase clave purists, clave can be written as a one-bar phrase in common time.) It is common to see most "salsa" music written in cut time. And some Afro-Cuban music has been written in 2/4. You will find that most of this book is written in cut time. The reason is quite simple; many of the patterns are easier to read in cut than in common time. But most importantly, and over-riding any discussion of notation or technique, is feel. The bottom line is, how does your playing feel. Keep that in mind as you learn from this book and CD.

Musicians from Santiago de Cuba (© Susanne Moss)

A HISTORY OF THE PAILITAS CUBANAS

Pailas Cubanas (© Susanne Moss)

The drums that most of us know as timbales have a very rich history. In Cuba, timbales are known by many different names. Pailitas cubanas, pailas cubanas, pailas, pailitas, timbaletas, panderetas, bongó, timbales; all of these names have been and are still used in Cuba. The most common name, used in most if not all parts of Cuba, is bongó! For clarity we will refer to the instrument either as timbales or pailitas Cubanas.

What of the roots of timbales? Not surprisingly, some people believe that the first drum was in the form of a tympani, formed from the trunk of a tree and animal skin. Famed Afro-Cuban musicologist Fernando Ortiz has said that the word "timbal" is of onomatopoeic origin, that the sound of the drums are similar to the name of the drum.

(Imagine the sound from a pair of tympani, first high than low. Can you hear the sounds "tim-bal"?) The name is also derived from the Arabic drums named "tabl" which the Spanish, after the Moorish invasions, called "atabal." In Cuba, the name became tamballe, then timbal. (Asia Minor had drums with names such as "tabl-sami," "tabl-al gawig," and the "table migri." These drums were also relatives of the tympani.)

Even farther back in time, the roots of timbales can be traced to Assyria, Asia Minor, and even India. In the ancient Sanskrit writing of India there are mentions of a great tympani-type instrument with a tight skin, a system of metal hooks for tuning, played with two curved sticks. In the eighth century, during the Crusades, contact was initiated between the Iberian Peninsula (Spain and Portugal) and the Moors of Northern Africa. This, in association with the conquest of the Byzantine Empire by the Turks, helped to bring the tympani to Europe.

Most musicologists agree that the tympani of Europe are one of the antecedents of modern day timbales. The Spanish word for tympani is tímpano or timbal. It is known that in Europe in 1670 tympani were incorporated as pairs for the first time. (Curt Sachs, [Ortiz] believes that the first tympani in Europe were used in the 14th Century.) The next date of great importance, according to Laureano Fuentes in his book Las Artes de Santiago de Cuba (The Arts of Santiago de Cuba), is 1852 when, for the first time, tympani were played in Cuba. They were played in Santiago de Cuba, in an Italian opera, Donizzetti's "Lucia di Lamermoor," and were played by Antonio Boza.

Cuban-style tympani were first played in the eastern parts of Cuba's "Oriente" provinces, principally in Holguín and Manzanillo. They were often found in the organ groups that were famous in that region. Tympani were also found in circuses.

In Los Instrumentos de la Musica Afrocubana Vol. IV, Ortiz describes the "paila," which many musicians nowadays use as another name for timbales or for a musical direction as to when to play the cáscara pattern. According to the writer Pichardo, paila is a vessel of iron or copper in the shape of half an orange. These vessels were used in the sugar cane factories and were used to hold guarapo or the juice of the cane. They were also used to fashion the Cuban tympani. In many cases, only one paila was used because one drum was more portable. It was up to the musical technique of the pailero to get all the sounds necessary for the various musical genres. The instrument was played with sticks and most of the time the pailero had to use his hand to assist in either producing a deep tone or a sharp note. The free hand would provide tension to the head which was played with

Notice the Tympani

the stick. There was no macho or hembra as there are with timbales today, and according to Carlos Borbolla, an organist and pailero from the early twentieth century, "one timbal alone must handle the acoustic endeavors of both sexes." In the Eastern provinces of Cuba, up until this century, musical groups consisting of an organ, a guayo (a large güiro), and a pailero made their music in the streets or at dances for

Organ Group with Pailero

the lower classes of Cubans.

The oldest of these pailas or vessels of copper were taken to Africa in the fifteenth century and were used as musical instruments in Guinea as well as by the people called mayombe. Ortiz believes that the Africans were trying to imitate the Europeans who had brought the instruments to the continent. In Zaire, for example, the inhabitants copied the timbales (remember that these are what we know of as tympani) and also the costumes and finery worn by the musicians, who were often soldiers.

Soldiers and the military have often had great influence over musical styles in many parts of the world. Drums have always been used, in one way or another, with the military. The earliest Cuban musicians who played in bands mostly came from the military, having been trained as musicians in the military battalions of the day. There was a racial distinction in the military battalions; the black battalions being called "pardo," and the black and white battalions "moreno." The orchestras of the day reflected this racial distinction, which was maintained by the Spanish military. The influences in the "pardo" battalions and their bands took the form of the inclusion of guiros and rhythmic patterns and improvisations performed by the timbalero (tympani-player).

Military Battalion with Tympani

danza, and danzón. During this time there were great economic problems in Cuba and drums the size and composition of the European style tympani were not possible to make. Drummers used the same calderos or pailas in which was manufactured sweets or guarapo as the basis of some of their adaptations of the European tympani. Goat skin was also used. The resulting drums were in various sizes but they were easier to make and easier to transport. These were called pailas.

Ortiz had some very interesting ideas about the origins of modern day timbales. He believes that bongoes are part of the antecedents of timbales. One reason for these roots is that the bongoes were held together with a center piece, as are our timbales. The bongoes were also played seated. And lastly, the bongoes had one head and were open on the bottom. Ortiz also believes that these instruments evolved from of all places the kitchen. At some time in Cuban history, sartenes (frying pans) were covered with skin, probably that of a goat, and tensioned with either rope or screws of some type, connected to a rim. These drums were also played with one stick and one hand. The word paila has as its derivatives the antique French word "paele" which in turn comes from the Latin "patella": a kind of fountain or metal plate. In modern French, "poele" means frying pan ("sarten" in Spanish).

A very important link in the chain of percussive events which brought us the pailitas cubanas are the timbalitos found in

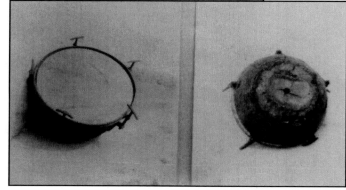
Orquesta Típica with Tympani

Cuba. They were called timbalitos because they resembled small tim-

How does what we know of as timbales today emerge from the tympani? In the early part of the twentieth century there was a great demand for the tympani due to the popularity of certain types of music in Cuba. Among these kinds of music were contradanza,

Old Style Pailas Cubanas from Matanzas, Cuba

bales, or tympani. They were made of wood

and most probably were small barrels, cut in two, and held olives imported into Cuba from Andalucia. Goat skin was nailed to the wider of the two openings. Now, the pailero could comfortably sit and play an instrument much smaller than the tympani. Also, the two drums could now be mounted together instead of on

Notice the Wood Drums

separate tripods.

The next generation of timbales were smaller and allowed the performer to sit and place the drums somewhat between his legs. The pailitas were seen as "children" to the European tympani and the Cuban pailas. The drums were also set up on a tripod, not separately as the tympani were played. In the first part of the twentieth century, pailitas cubanas began to make their appearance as the orquesta típica (which played many types of music like contradanza and danza) began to fade and be replaced by the charanga or charanga francesa, which played more danzon and danzonete (and later, chachachá). Even in the organ groups of the eastern provinces, pailitas cubanas began to replace the larger timbale or tympani.

The author respectfully submits this hypothesis. In the very early twentieth century, Cuban families who could afford to sent their musically talented children to the United States to learn the new American music, jazz. Jazz at that time included many different styles of music, like fox trot, charleston, and other styles. The Cuban musicians would then return to Cuba to perform at dances for the upper class. Also performing at these dances were the orquestas típicas. The drummers in the jazz bands had a small trap set, most probably bass drum, snare drum, cymbal, perhaps woodblock and cowbell, and a "chinese" tom. The

timbalero in the orchestra played tympani. If you were playing a larger drum like tympani, wouldn't you perhaps investigate the "other" drummer's trap set, looking at the small snare drum, perhaps playing it to hear how it sounded without snares? Perhaps this is one of the first inspirations to "downsize" the Cuban tympani, making the pailitas more like a snare drum with one head. And then there were the cowbells and woodblock so common with the early American trap set. Another inspiration for the pailero? Perhaps.

The First Cuban Jazz Band

Cuban percussionists developed different styles of playing first the tympani then the pailitas cubanas or timbales. The Cubans used their hands and fingers to produce sound, a technique called "manoseo del cuero." Also, as a forerunner of cáscara, Cuban drummers would play on the shell or cáscara of the tympani. They also would more commonly play on the rim or "border" of the tympani. The left hand would keep time on the hembra, the larger of the two tympanis. This sound was used during specific sections of songs, a forerunner to modern timbales, when, for example, cáscara is typically used for verses. The sound of baqueteo was also first developed on the tympani where simultaneous beats were produced by a stick on the head or cáscara while the fingers produced another sound, filling in where one hand did not play.

As you can see, timbales as we know them have a long and very interesting history. All the way from Africa and India, with influences from Europe and North America, playing Cuban timbales is an art well worth learning.

SETTING UP THE TIMBALES

Old Style Timbales with Macho on Right

Timbales come in many sizes and are made out of many different types of materials. The most popular sizes are the 14" and 15" drums. Another popular pair of sizes are 13" and 14". Timbalitos are also manufactured. They are smaller than the 13" and 14" drums and have a higher pitched sound. Recently there has been great interest, from players and manufacturers alike, in mini-timbales or drum set timbales, ranging in size from 6" to 10". They can be used in a variety of settings.

Changuito uses 14" and 15" drums. He also has used drums called timbalones which are quite a bit deeper than the regular timbales. Timbalones are commonly used in the typical charanga orchestras.

Timbales can be made of stainless steel. Brass timbales are also common. Other materials, such as wood, may also be used. Each shell material has its own distinctive cáscara and drum sound. Changuito uses steel drums.

Brass Timbales

Setting up drums is a very personal thing; each of us have our own ideas about how to do it. There are several facts about timbales which are very important to know and which may help you when you are setting up.

The larger drum (hembra) is the low drum (mellower tone) and the smaller drum (macho) is the high drum with a sharper tone. The reason given for the naming of the drums is interesting. With many drums of African origin, there is a sexualization, where one drum or the other (when in pairs) has certain male or female characteristics. The mellower tone of the hembra corresponds to the mellower characteristics of the female, while the macho has a more aggressive "personality" and a much more assertive tone.

The two drums are set up with the smaller drum (macho) set up to the right-handed player's right. The larger drum (hembra) is on the left. This is a very important point when setting up your drums. Setting up this way makes it easier to play the hembra while playing cáscara or bell. The drums should be positioned so the rim shot on the macho is easy to play. This is an important part of your vocabulary and it is very important for you to be able to play this comfortably.

The center post of most timbales is where you would mount cowbells, wood blocks, and

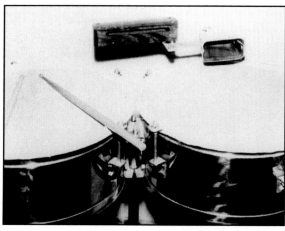

Old Setup of Cha-Cha Bell and Woodblock

other items. There does not seem to be any "stock" set up for bells, etc. Here is a very typical way of setting up two bells. The "mambo" bell is set up with the mouth facing the right of the right-handed player. (The mambo bell can be used for many different styles of Afro-Cuban music.) The chacha bell is set up so that the mouth of the bell is easily accessible.

If a bass drum is to be used, it should also be set up so it can be played comfortably.

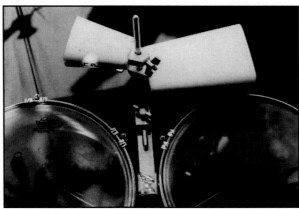

If a cymbal is to be set up, it is most common to find it in the position featured in the photograph. It should be easy to reach. Which

type of cymbal to use? Some cymbal companies are now manufacturing cymbals specifically made for playing with "latin" grooves. These cymbals have a prominent bell sound with a lot of definition afforded by the body of the cymbal. They can also be crashed. As with drums and bells, the choice is a personal one.

TUNING THE TIMBALES

Amadito Valdés and Jóse Sanchez, both wonderful Afro-Cuban percussionists, agree that tuning the two drums a fourth apart is the most effective method. Changuito, ever the non-conformist, disagrees and says that a fifth is the way to go. Maximiliana Jaquinet, in her scholarly paper "*Approximación a las Pailas Cubanas,*" writes that tuning of a fourth or fifth apart is common. Whichever route you choose to go, tuning is accomplished very easily on most modern timbales by using a wrench of appropriate size to turn bolts which are inserted into lugs on the shells.

The predecessors of today's drums were tuned in assorted ways. They could have tuning keys which the player would manually turn, much like their tympani ancestors. Some, like the timbalitos, had the goat skin tacked on to the wooden shells. And still others were tuned by holding them close to a fire.

Tuning modern timbales can be accomplished in many ways. First tighten each tensioning rod (usually some kind of bolt) so that the drum is in tune with itself. The head is properly seated when, after a few turns of each tensioning rod, the drum produces a tone when the head is struck. Then begin at one bolt and, tightening an eighth of a turn, proceed in a clock-wise fashion around the drum. When I have had my own questions about tuning I have just listened to my favorite percussionists and copied their tuning. On the accompanying CD you have a great opportunity to listen to Changuito's tuning and copy it!

Amadito Valdés

José Sanchez

NOTATION KEY

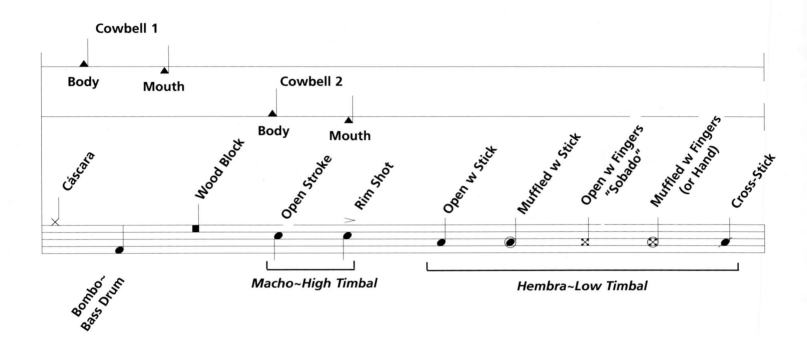

Note: When a particular style requires only one cowbell, only one line is shown above the staff, with instructions or an indication of which bell to play (i.e. chacha bell, mambo bell, bongo bell). When a style requires two bells there is one line corresponding to each bell. Some examples also include an additional reduced staff above each example showing the direction of the clave.

SOUNDS OF THE TIMBALES

The sound of the shell, or *cáscara*, is a very important part of the overall sound of the timbales. This sound is used typically, in salsa-style songs, during verses, piano solos, solos by other instruments as indicated in the musical directions, and in other musical sections. The sound is also found in other types of Afro-Cuban song styles. The sound is dry and crisp with a bright attack. The metal used to make the timbales has a lot to do with the sound. Steel and brass are the most common metals used to make timbales and each gives a distinctive flavor to the cáscara.

The cáscara is written on the top line of the staff.

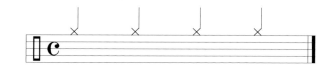

The *macho*, or smaller of the two drums, has two main sounds available to you. One of the most important sounds from the macho is the rim shot. This sound is one of the most recognized timbale tones. It is achieved by striking, with sufficient force, the head and rim simultaneously evoking a sharp, bright and somewhat resonant tone. Since this is such an important feature of the timbales, you should take the time to make sure that the height of your drums is adjusted so that striking the rim shot is consistent.

The rim shot on the macho is written on the third space of the staff with an accent mark.

Another sound from the macho is the open tone. You don't want to use this drum just for rim shots! Very typically, the macho is struck with the stick, not with an open hand. (The hembra can be played this way, as we will learn later.)

The *hembra*, or low drum, also has several sounds available for you. It is very, very rare to play rim shots, as in the macho, on the hembra. More commonly, the open tone of the drum is used. This sound can be achieved by playing with a stick. You don't have to strike the drum very hard to achieve a good tone. If the drum is tuned correctly the open tone should sing out when skin is struck with stick.

Counting from the bottom up, the hembra is written in the second space of the staff.

Open tones on the hembra can also be achieved by striking the skin with the hand or finger, or fingers. This method is usually used when the other hand is playing another pattern on the drums, i.e. cáscara, or bell patterns.

Changuito's main method for achieving the open tone on the hembra is to gently stroke it, while cradling the stick in the crook of the thumb and forefinger. This may take some getting used to but this is the primary way Changuito gets this sound. One of the variations is using the middle and fourth finger fingers to achieve this sound.

Cuban drummers name this sound *soba-do*. The way this was described to me was that when you have a stomachache and your mom rubs some salve on your stomach, the motion used is the Spanish verb sobar. It means to rub or massage.

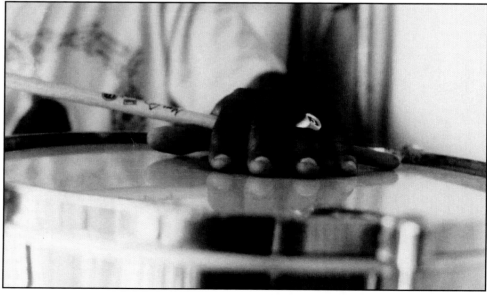

Changuito Plays Sobado

A Short History of the Cowbell

Why does the timbalero play cowbell, or in some cases, cowbells of various sizes? There are various stories about the roots of the cowbell, but none as interesting as the story about Antonio Orta Ferrol, also known as "Menengue." Menengue was a very famous timbalero in Cuba in the very early 20th century. There is no mention in the story whether Menengue played timbales (as we know them) or the Cuban pailas (tympani). In a book by Leonardo Padura Fuentes (Ediciones Union, 1994), the author writes that in 1912, before he left for a job with a dance band, Menengue was asked by his mother to buy a bell for their cow. Ever the abiding son, he did what he was told and placed the bell in a sack. On his way to the job, Menegue got quite drunk as was his custom. At the gig, things got hot and heavy. Well, it seems that at the height of musical passion, probably more than slightly intoxicated, Menegue reached into the sack, brought out the bell and proceeded to play it, just as if he had always done it that way. This situation occurred in the orchestra led by the flautist Tata Alfonso. The pianist in the orchestra was Antonio María Romeu, a very famous Cuban musician. This story was told to me by more than one person.

Antonio Orta Ferrol, "Menengue"

Another story is told by Jóse Sanchez. Jóse says that one timbalero, by mistake, hit a cowbell in the montuno section of a danzon. And the new sound was liked by everyone in the orquesta tipica. He says another story is that a timbalero forgot his wood block. One of the musicians in the band happened to have a cowbell (perhaps he too had purchased one for a cow!) and he lent it to the timbalero. He used it, everyone liked it, and the cowbell stayed.

Amadito Valdes says that it may have been the great timbalero, Ulpiano Diaz, who first played cowbell. Changuito says it may have been another great, Guillermo Garcia. Whatever the story, the cowbells are a very important part of the timbale set-up.

There seems to be no set method for the placement of cowbells with timbales. Changuito's set-up for this book and CD uses two bells, a "mambo" style bell and a chacha bell. The mambo style bell has more possibilities of sound than a bell of similar size, the bongo bell. The bongo bell is used by the bongocero (bongo player) during specific sections of Afro-Cuban songs. The construction of the bells—thickness of metal, shape of the bell— seems to have a lot to do with the tonal possibilities. Changuito uses the full range of sounds available from the mambo bell as well as from the chacha bell. He also changes the positioning of the bells for different styles

José Sanchez's Setup

of music. (He doesn't change them during gigs, which leads me to believe he may use different set-ups for different gigs.) Most of the time I have seen him, his set-up allowed him to play two different sounds on each bell, the mouth of the bell, and the body of the bell.

One of Changuito's Cowbell Arrangements

In this example we can hear the two different tones of the mambo bell, written on different spaces of the staff.

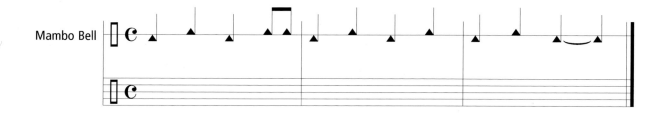

The chacha bell is the smaller of the two bells. Typically, this bell is used to play rhythms like chachachá. Changuito's set up uses the chacha bell in this manner but Changuito uses this bell in many other ways. He uses both mouth and body of bell to achieve two distinct tones and also uses these tones in various rhythmic patterns.

Here are the two tones, once again written on two spaces in the staff.

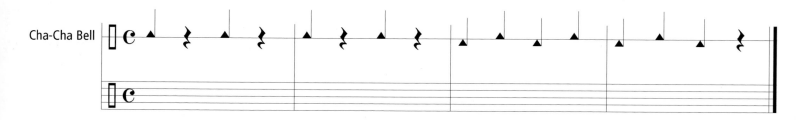

THE CLAVE

The clave is a Cuban instrument. Fernando Ortiz stated in 1928 that in all the ethnographic museums he visited he did not find an instrument like the clave. In the chapter on clave in Ortiz's *Los Instrumentos de la Music Afrocubana* he details how though searching in Europe, Africa, and in other locations, he could not find any mention of clave or any history of such an instrument. He found the "rhythmic cells" which may define la clave, but could not find the actual instrument. There are many examples of instruments made from wood in African cultures but the clave is uniquely Cuban.

The word clavija means "pin" or "peg." It has been thought that laborers who used to load and unload ships in the harbors of Havana and other Cuban ports made instruments from the pieces of rigging that which looked like large wooden pins or pegs. (Ropes were sometimes attached to these pegs.) This may be one way that clave got its name. The name for both sticks that make up the instrument is "la clave," the clave.

There are no other (or they are rarely encountered) instruments where the player must cup one of the pair of claves in one hand (for a more amplified sound) and then strike this with the other. (This, by the way, is the proper technique for playing clave. By cupping one's hand, placing one wooden clave in

because they both are equal partners in the sound produced when hembra is struck by macho. As a percussion instrument (in the family of idiophones) this is a rare occurrence and gives the clave an important structure.

Ortiz calls the clave the spirit of the melody! The feeling of the clave in Cuba is much more than just a rhythm, two pieces of wood being struck together. It is life. It is a symphony. It is one of the most important things about being Cuban. As Ortiz says, "the clave, as it goes out into the world, will sweeten everyone's life much more than the sugar from Cuba's cane fields."

The clave, like many other instruments of African origin, has been "sexualized." Each part is either male or female, macho or hembra. There is a female (the deeper, mellower toned wood) and a male, which generates the higher pitched tone. Sometimes the mellower toned piece of wood, the hembra, is carved out a bit to enhance the sound quality. The macho does the striking, in order to produce a mellow tone from the hembra.

There are two clave patterns, the son clave and the rumba clave, both illustrated above. These two clave patterns vary only in one note, but this variation definitely gives each its own swing, or feeling. Try this simple exercise. Tap both feet on the downbeats (in cut time this would be on "1" and "2") and

the hand and then striking, a more mellifluous tone is generated.) Montadón, cited by Ortiz, talks about how important the clave is as an instrument. He writes that both "bodies," both pieces of the clave are of balanced importance

play the son clave. Feel the way the pattern works with the downbeats. Now, play the rumba clave and notice the difference between the two.

The clave rhythm may begin on either the first or second measure of the pattern. The different directions of the clave are commonly referred to as 3-2 and 2-3 direction. These are also called forward (3-2) and reverse (2-3) clave directions. The direction of the clave determines the feel of the music being played. (Again you could try the simple exercise as above, but this time first play the clave—either rumba or son—in forward direction. Stop the clave, wait for a few moments, and then try the same clave in the "other" direction. Notice and feel the difference.) It is commonplace to overemphasize the technical aspects of clave. This is the most important concept of Afro-Cuban music but do not overemphasize it and then forget about the feel of the music.

Written here is an example of how, even starting in the forward direction of son clave, one can "change the direction" of a musical composition. Very simply, we have started our "composition" in son clave, 3-2 direction. By playing a three bar phrase and inserting repeat signs, our "composition" has now "changed" to the 2-3 direction. (Think of the new 2-3 section as a different section of our song.) But the clave never changed. The composition changed around the clave!

CLAVE RELATED HAND EXERCISES AND WARMUPS

Changuito uses various patterns to warm up. Presented are four which can also be used as jump off points for solo ideas. These patterns are based on the rumba clave, perhaps giving you an insight as to how Changuito develops his ideas. If his warm up exercises reflect this most basic of Afro-Cuban phrases, most probably many other solo phrases are constructed similarly, reflecting basic phrases with a lot of feel. Changuito then uses his artistic mastery to develop these basic ideas into incredible solo passages.

Clave Hand Exercise 1

This pattern uses alternating single strokes to make an interesting and challenging pattern. As you can see, the pattern is played all on the macho. Don't be fooled by thinking that this is just singles with some accents. There are sections which may prove difficult. The last note of the 2nd sextuplet, measures 2, 4, and 6, can really be difficult due to the accented left hand. This needs to be practiced slowly at first.

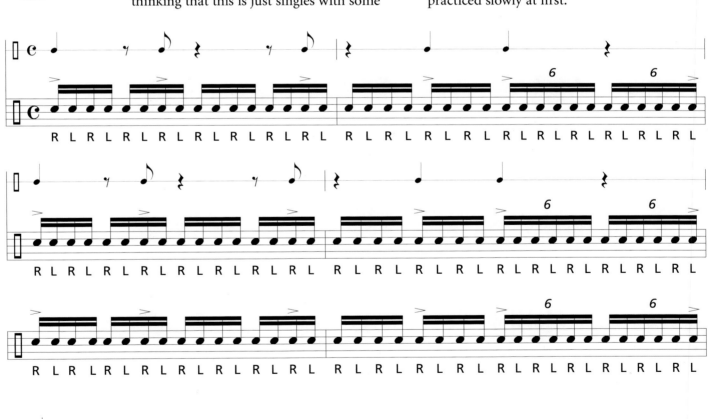

Clave Hand Exercise 2

The hembra is now added on that accented note within the sextuplet.

Slowly, carefully, practice until you can feel the clave.

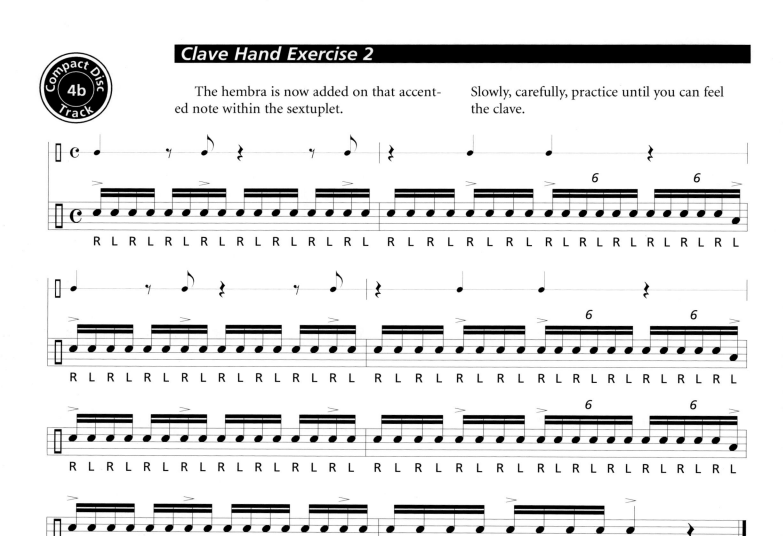

Clave Hand Exercise 3

Again based on clave and first played just on the macho, this phrase utilizes an interesting sticking pattern.

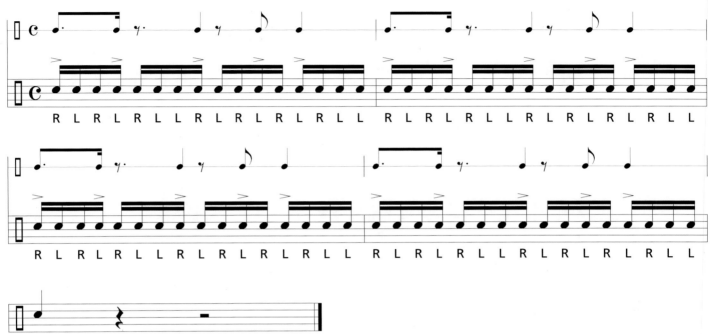

Clave Hand Exercise 4

The same phrase, with the hembra now also involved.

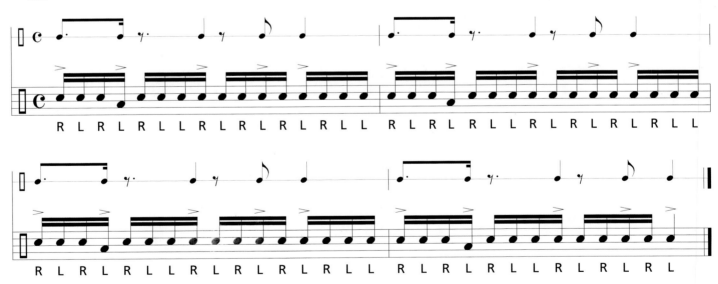

Danzón

The danzón is one of the first examples of popular music in Cuba. It has its roots in European danza and contradanza, which were traditionally played, percussion-wise, using tympani (pailas cubanas). These tympani, the Cuban style, were much smaller than their European cousins. The pailitas cubanas, or timbales as we call them, were developed partly as an answer to the need for a portable instrument to bring this "refined" style of Cuban music to perhaps less accessible areas in and around Havana, Santiago de Cuba and other areas in Cuba. Traditional tympani were too cumbersome to carry by mule or horseback.

From as early as the eighteenth century there are references of the arrival of French ships to the island of Cuba. The arrival of these ships, with their French crew and others on board, greatly influenced the customs and esthetics of Cuban culture. These influences were enhanced by the migration of French colonists from Haiti, after the successful slave revolution (the first record of this movement being in 1789). Another great influence was the arrival in Cuba of French colonists from Louisiana, after Napoleon Bonaparte sold Louisiana as part of the Louisiana Purchase in 1812. Musically, the French "contradanza" or "country dance" and the minuet were two of the most important French "imports." The contradanza was very quickly "Cubanized" and became the favorite dance of many Cubans, especially those in the upper classes. The French colonists were in the mountainous Eastern regions of Cuba but the country-dance had no problems reaching all areas of Cuba including the dance halls of Havana.

There existed in Cuba two contradanzas, the Oriental (from the Eastern provinces) and the Habanera (from Havana and surrounding areas). The Oriental was more popular, which caused a lot of problems. After all, Havana was the capital!

The African influence on the contradanza is very important because this influence gave birth to what is known as Cuban music. The way of dancing the contradanza, the men and women in a double line with couples facing each other, was a style very familiar to the African slaves. It was how many Africans danced in their home countries. This fact is very important because it helped greatly in the "acceptance" of the music by a majority of the Cuban population. Also, parts of certain contradanzas (and later forms called the danza) were written and performed in 6/8. This addition of the 6/8 time signature may be the first heard influence of African music on European music. Cuban music was born! The oldest Cuban contradanza known is titled "San Pascual Bailon" and was created in 1803.

The danza is not anything else but a continuation of this musical phenomenon. By 1842, composers were beginning to add lyrics to the contradanza, singing them in the Habanera style. Composers of danzas, most notably Ignacio Servantes, used rich harmonies and great rhythmic figures to embellish their arrangements. The style of contradanza and danza gave birth to the danzón. The danzón is slower than the genres that preceded it. Much more appropriate for the tropical Cuban climate! Danzón is considered the Cuban national dance.

Cuban contradanzas were initially played by orquestas típicas which consisted of two violins, two clarinets, a contrabass, a "cornetín" (a trumpet-like instrument), a trombone, "pailas cubanas" (tympani), and güiro. The charanga francesa, or orquestas francesas, or simply charangas, are direct descendants of the orquestas típicas. Whereas the clarinet played in these orquestas típicas, its part was taken over by the flute (the Cuban wood flute, with Haitian roots, with five keys and a high register) in the charanga francesa. The metales (horns) are replaced in the charanga francesa by the violins. The danzón also featured, in the song's first movement, elements of the son, the most important and influential music from the Eastern part of Cuba.

Miguel Faílde is the inventor of the danzón. Faílde was born in Guamarcaro, Matanzas, Cuba in 1852. The first danzón was performed January 1, 1879 in the Liceo de Matanzas. Its name is "*Las Alturas de Simpson*." Faílde died in 1920.

Las Alturas de Simpson
The First Danzón

We begin the study of timbales with danzón because from the music, rhythm, and dance of danzón emerged many, if not all of the popular Cuban music styles, most assuredly chachachá and possibly mambo. The son, which came from the Eastern regions of Cuba (Oriente province and possibly others), had a great influence also on Cuban music and its merging with the danzón provided the emphasis for many new and exciting styles.

Changuito has many, many different ways of playing danzón. Here are three examples which will give you a good idea of the rhythm of danzón on timbales. Not only is there a main rhythm to the danzón, there is a way to "stick" the rhythm on timbales. The sticking is written for you. Changuito uses various methods to strike the drum, with sticks playing open tones, rim shots, and muffled strokes. Sometimes he uses his fingers to play the muffled strokes. Following the notation and listening to the accompanying CD will clearly demonstrate the danzón.

The basic danzón pattern gives you a basic idea of the rhythm. Our advice, which is repeated throughout this book, is to practice each pattern extremely slow, perhaps out of time, to get a feel for the sticking involved. Some patterns may be a bit easier than others.

The second measures of all the danzones contain a left hand pattern which serves basically as a time keeper. The left hand plays the "deadened pattern with fingers" on most of the "ands" of beats 1, 2, and 3. Although Changuito plays most of them, only the most important, and heard, notes have been transcribed.

Note: The notation of the muffled hembra played with a stick, is a simplified way of notating the actual sound. This sound is played by striking the hembra with one stick while the other hand is deadening the hembra.

Preliminary Exercises~Combining the Sounds from the Timbales

These sections, found in each chapter, will concentrate on getting you used to playing the timbales for each of the rhythms being studied. There are various movements with which you will need to familiarize yourself when learning these rhythms on timbales. We have already looked at and listened to the basic sounds available from the drums and bells. These exercises look at some combinations of sounds and the sticking patterns and independence they involve. Repeat each short phrase as many times as necessary in order to develop proper technique and the proper sounds from the instrument.

The first rhythm in the book is that of danzón. Danzón uses some interesting sounds and hand patterns. The muffled hembra and cross stick in the hembra is played using a sticking pattern very similar to the right paradiddle. Here is the pattern as it is played on the hembra. First, a muffled sound is played on the hembra with stick. The muffled sound is achieved by leaving the left hand lying on the drum while you strike the drum, in the center, with the right stick. This sound is followed by a cross stick in the hembra with the left stick. Following this sound are two more muffled hembra sounds. Let's try this pattern.

This next pattern begins with a left cross stick on the hembra, followed by a muffled hembra with the right hand. The next sound is new: the open hembra, played with the right stick. Following the open sound is another cross stick with left hand.

Pattern 3 features four different sounds from the hembra. Muffled hembra with right stick is followed by muffled hembra with fingers of the left hand. The open sound, right stick, is next, followed by a left cross stick. Each of these patterns needs to be practiced many times to feel the flow necessary for the actual danzón.

Pattern four has five different sounds from both drums. A muffled hembra, right hand, is followed by an accented macho. This accent sound is very important! Following the accented macho is another muffled hembra, right hand, followed by hembra muffled with hand or fingers, left hand. An open hembra and cross stick round out the measure.

Correct execution of these four patterns will lead you to a better understanding of the hand movements necessary for danzón.

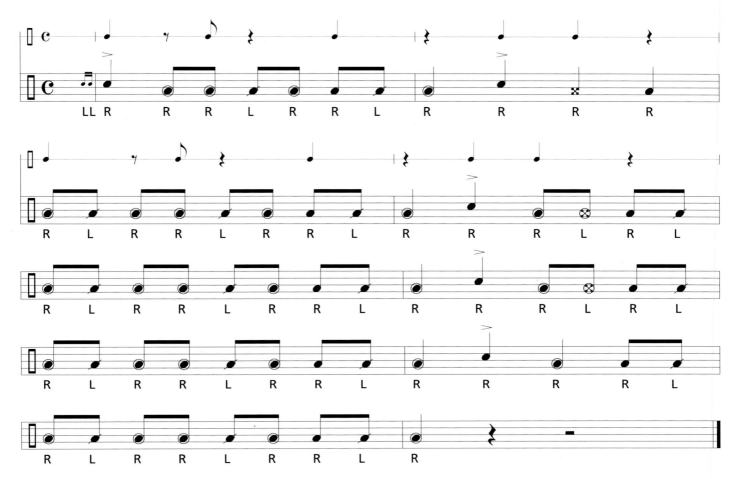

Danzón~Example 1

Variations one and two add some open tones and rim shots to spice up the danzón. These still fall into a typical category and are very important to learn. Striving for feel is the most important concept for this and everything else in this book.

Danzón~Example 2

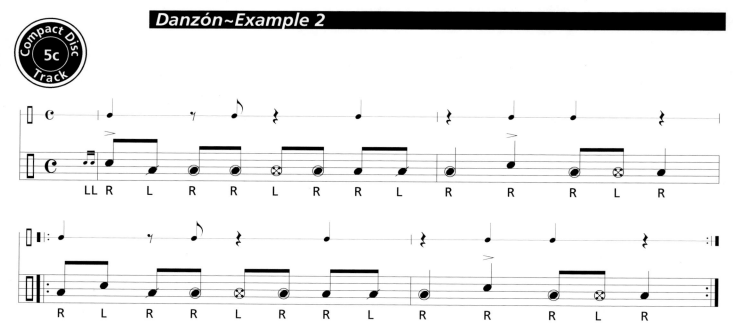

ABANICO

The Spanish word abanico means fan, as in ceiling fan, attic fan or something with which to fan yourself. It seems to come from the fans that were used, and in some cases still are used, in the dancing of classic Cuban dances like the contradanza, danza, and danzón. Each section of the dance, from introduction of the partners to the actual dance itself, had special accompanying music played for the section. One section of a dance called for the participating ladies to all open their fans at a certain time. These fans are traditionally made of wooden slats. Imagine the sound, if you will, of dozen of these fans opening simultaneously. A drummer, who history has perhaps consigned to anonymity, thought of this sound and came up with the abanico on timbales,

signifying the change between sections of Afro-Cuban songs. In "Las Pailitas Cubanas" by Marta Rodriguez Cuervo, the abanico is referred to as "a roll which called for the beginning of the improvisational section of the danzón."

In salsa-style tunes, the abanico has been used extensively to signal the change between the verse section and the chorus section of a song. (It can also be used in other ways but this way is very basic to the style.) The abanico is also used in chachachá and other forms of Afro-Cuban music. Changuito uses the abanico in traditional and non-traditional ways. We feel that it is most important for you to learn this important part of playing the timbales.

Abanico for Chachachá

The abanico is comprised of two sounds, the crack of the rim shot (there are two separate rim shots) and the dry roll in the macho. As you can see in the next example, the accented notes in the macho are very important for the abanico. This is a very basic abanico.

As you listen to more and more Afro-Cuban music you will hear others. With this basic idea you will be able to interpret the other, more advanced patterns. Practice slowly at first, increasing the tempo only when you feel comfortable.

Abanico and Traditional Danzón with Bell

Here is an example of the abanico in use with the traditional danzón with chacha bell. It is one of the forerunners of the chacha bell pattern.

Cha-Cha Bell

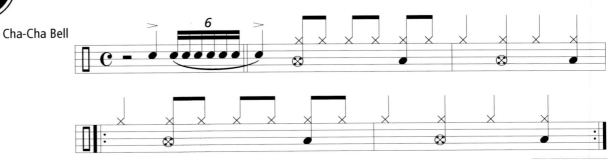

CHACHACHÁ

Enrique Jorrín is credited by many as the inventor of chachachá. The dance gets its name, according to Jorrín, from the sound of the dancers' feet on the dance floor. In 1951 Jorrín used the sound of a very typical Afro-Cuban style band, called charanga francesa, along with what were called danzones de nuevo ritmo (danzons of new rhythm) to help create this new Afro-Cuban popular dance feel.

An important feature of this new dance was the utilization of a new rhythms and the addition of vocals and choruses. One of the most important new rhythms and a very important part for the timbalero is the cha-cha bell. It is a driving pattern and a very "up" feel. The feel is enhanced by playing all of the eighth notes within the pattern, with the downbeats being accented.

Once again, the hembra plays a very important part, emphasizing the tumbao of the tumbadoras (congas) and bass. Don't underestimate this part. It is most important.

Preliminary Exercises

The accented attack on the macho is very important. It is also very important to be able to make the transition from this sound to the sound of either cowbell. This transition is very important with several different rhythms and patterns. Here is the transition for you to practice. First with the chacha bell.

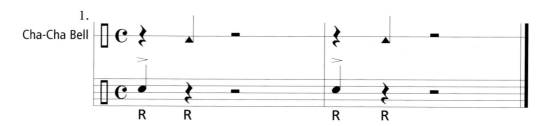

Now with the mambo bell. (*Note 1: Even though the mambo bell is not usually used in chachachá, Changuito felt that it was important to include this information here.*) (*Note 2: At times it is easier to write the different bells (chacha and mambo) on the same line, when they are used in separate exercises. Whenever this happens you will be notified by accompanying text.*)

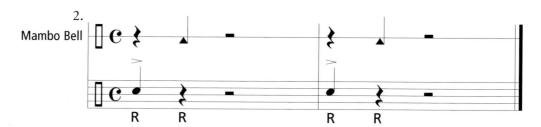

The interplay of bell and drums, especially hembra, is very important when learning Afro-Cuban timbales. Here's an illustration of that interplay with chacha bell and hembra.

You will be playing two sounds on the cha-cha bell (mouth and body) while the left hand plays the hembra muffled with hand or fingers.

3.

Now the open hembra is added, played with a "flick" of the fingers of the left hand. (*Note: Please re-read "How to Practice this Book" for important tips on getting the most from these basic exercises.*)

4.

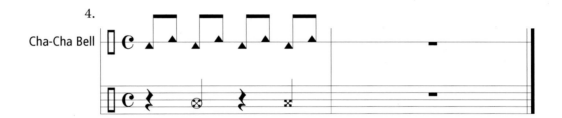

Campana/Cha-Cha Bell Examples

Here is the chacha bell playing all eighths, while accenting the downbeat.

1.

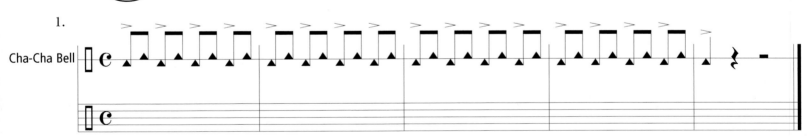

Now a basic chachachá. Notice the simple and basic closed and open tone in the hembra.

2.

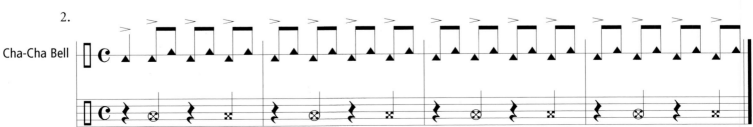

When the music really starts to groove, the montuno (sometimes translated as a two-bar piano vamp) is smoking' and the flute is really blowing, the timbalero is affected by what is happening around him or her (both by the band and by the dancers), the excitement is shown in the hembra. The timbalero (timbale player) may add more notes or play a different pattern in the hembra.

There is a long history of the relationship between the drum and the flute. As far back as 2,000 years ago, an author, writing in the ancient writing of the Periplo de Hannon, stated that sailors sailing down the African coast could, at night, hear a great noise made by drums, flutes, and cymbals. Also, a Roman writer named Pomponio Mela wrote of a place inhabited by satyrs, where it was quiet during the day but at night one could see bonfires and the superhuman sound of drums, cymbals, and flutes. Perhaps this gives you an idea of the history of the relationship and how special it really is!

This type of playing the open tone does not occur on a frequent basis but the timbalero, being affected by the montuno, the flute, the dancers, etc., can show the effect by playing a bit more in the hembra, all the while maintaining the groove. (Measures 8-10 are good examples of this.) It may happen only one time during a song, after which the timbalero reverts back to playing a basic groove in the hembra. This musical example demonstrates how emotion and excitement can affect Changuito's playing, as well as your own!

3.

Cha-Cha Bell

The mixture of congas and timbales, the tumbao of the conga and the sobado in the hembra, is one of Cuban popular music's most influential and important sounds and feels. It is this mix, along with maracas, clave, and or/ guiro, that really makes the music swing. This example is of the basic chachachá accompanied by a simple one drum marcha in the conga. First you will hear the abanico. Pay attention to the important sounds and try to emulate them. Please listen to CD track 10.

MAMBO

What is this word, mambo? Many famous Cuban musicians have been asked this question and many music researchers have been trying to find out where it comes from, what it means, and more importantly, who invented the musical style called mambo. Manuel Cuellar Vizcaino, a famous Afro-Cuban scholar, says that he had never encountered the word in any books. Even famous musicians of his day (Antonio Arcano, for example) could not explain the birth of the name. Vizcaino says that Fernando Ortiz talks about the word "mamba," a district in Equatorial Africa. Also he has found the word "mombo," given to a slave in a certain African region. Obdulio Morales says that the word originates from a scream or yell which dancers shout during the hot sections of dance numbers. It is also an expression used by those who dance rumba columbia (one of the three types of rumba) and it signifies dancing ability and a feeling for the dance.

Arsenio Rodriguez, the great Cuban tres (Cuban style guitar) player and composer, stated that the word mambo was African in origin, from the Congolese dialect. He claimed its roots are in the conversation between vocalists where one says to the other, "abre cuto güirí mambo" or "open your ears and listen to what I want to say" (a very macho thing to say). Arsenio is one of the musicians who is credited with either inventing or greatly popularizing the mambo. He also was one of the first band leaders to add congas to a musical group. He said that he had to do something to unify the feeling of tension represented in the African phrase. The resultant new dance was called mambo.

Another great Cuban composer, Dámaso Pérez Prado, said that "mambo" was a Cuban word. When someone wanted to say that the situation was a good one, they would say "el mambo esta bien." Prado said that musically he didn't want to comment on who invented the dance. Just that "mambo" was a name, and that was it.

There are many that say that Dámaso Pérez Prado was the inventor of the mambo. He defined the characteristics of mambo as being very syncopated. The trumpets carry the melody, the bass accompanies, and this is combined with the bongoes and tumbas ("congas"). Prado did not mention timbales as they were not yet commonly used in Afro-Cuban dance bands of his era (late '30s and '40s). Interestingly, Dámaso Pérez Prado had to move to Mexico to invent the mambo. He claims in an interview that since he did not have the opportunity to play mambo in Cuba he went to Mexico.

A big difference between what Perez Prado did in the two countries was that he had written all the arrangements in Mexico whereas in Cuba only a bit would be written out. (There seems to have been a lot of freedom with the arrangements in Cuba!) This may have given him more opportunities, in Mexico, to write out more syncopated figures and more intricate arrangements. Dámaso Pérez Prado wrote his first mambos in 1949 in a record named José y Macamé. "Mambo numero 5" and "Mambo, que rico mambo" were two very famous songs from this recording.

Whereas the originators of many Cuban musical styles are known, the creator of the mambo seems to still be in question.

In order to play this musical style on timbales, you must know basic patterns. These patterns are the cáscara pattern and cowbell patterns. As with most musical styles with Cuban roots, these patterns change with time. You will find some very typical patterns in this section and you will find more modern patterns. For example, some of Changuito's cáscara patterns are definitely not "traditional," but they swing. Also, and very important for you to learn, are the two-bell patterns found later in this section. Bass drum is also added. Mastering this section will help you be ready for the next salsa gig that comes your way!

The shell of the drums is a very important sound. You have already heard how the shell sounds: crisp and dry. Later you will be asked to combined this crisp attack with the sound of the hembra. Here is a beginning lesson in making this combination. First we will combine three beats of the shell, or cáscara, with an open sound from the hembra, played with the fingers (or just the middle finger) of the left hand. You should be playing these cáscara sounds on the shell of the high drum (macho).

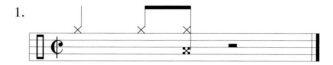

Now, inserted between two cáscara attacks, is the left hand playing the hembra muffled with hand or fingers.

There are two other basic movements involving these three sounds. With exercise three you are playing a different combination involving the dry sound of the cáscara with the hembra muffled with hand or fingers.

Pattern 4 has you playing an open sound from the hembra between two attacks from the shell of the high drum (macho).

We've already practiced making the transition from the accented macho to the mambo bell. Here are some exercises to get you accustomed to what the left hand plays on the hembra. Exercise five begins with the accented macho, transitioning to the body of the mambo bell with the same hand while the left hand plays the hembra muffled with hand or fingers.

Exercise six adds the open sound of the hembra. (*Note: As with all of these patterns, repetition is the key.*)

6.

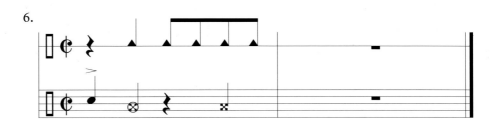

Here is another combination of mambo bell and hembra.

The open sound of the low drum is featured.

7.

Exercise eight adds the muffled hembra.

8.

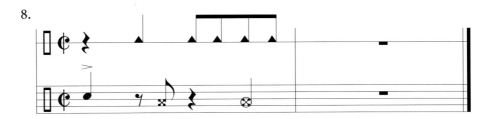

Changuito Playing Cáscara

The cáscara, in its many forms and variations, is one of the most basic and important patterns for you to learn on timbales. Cáscara, in Spanish, means shell, like the shell of the timbales. This is where it is played, although there are times when this pattern is also played on a cowbell or cymbal. When played on the shell, the sound is dry and crisp. It should sound like a wood stick on a metal shell. Imagine how that should sound. It will help you to achieve the correct tone.

Also, cáscara has to be played with an attitude. It's not a pattern to play laid back or lazy. It must have a certain drive to it. This is an unwritten rule that applies to many styles of Afro-Cuban music. There is an unmistakable drive and energy to the music. And this movement begins with you.

Where does the cáscara pattern come from? There are many versions of its inception. The cáscara is a pattern whose roots may be associated with the influence of American jazz bands in the early part of the 20th century. Amadito Valdes states this particular belief. The hi-hat and ride cymbal pattern could have influenced timbaleros of those days to develop their own syncopated timekeeping patterns.

Another influence on the development of the cáscara pattern could be that of the rumba. One of the palitos pattern for rumba is very near to the sound of the cáscara. If played with one hand, this pattern sounds identical to the cáscara. In a 1991 interview from Percussioni magazine, Tito Puente alludes to the fact that the cáscara comes from the rumba. Andy Gonzalez, the great bassist, also feels that the roots of cáscara are from rumba.

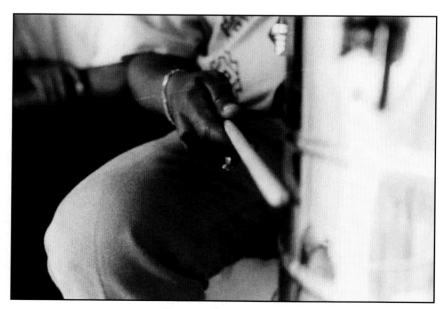

Close-up of Stick on Shell

The Palitos Pattern~one example of many

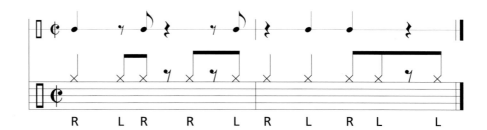

The Catá Pattern

The Catá

And yet another pattern, proffered by two great Cuban timbaleros, Jóse Manuel Sanchez and Yonder DeJesus Peña Llovet, might give us another clue to the origins of cáscara. The rhythm played by the catá in tumba francesa, a rhythm of the eastern part of Cuba, could be considered a close cousin to the cáscara. The rhythm is transcribed for you.

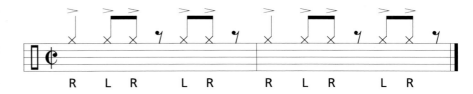

The Cinquillo Cubano

There is an important rhythm, developed in Cuba and heard in the danzón, called Cinquillo Cubano. This is a very important five note phrase. ("Cinco" in Spanish is "five.")

This rhythm is similar in notation to the catá pattern from tumba francesa and some Cuban percussionists feels that this might also have been an influence on the development of the cáscara. (*Note: The musical nota-* *tion which follows is an approximation of a tympani part for danzón. The notation is quoted from "Los Timbales," a work by Maria Elena Vinueza Gonzalez. The original was written in the 2/4 time signature. This notation does not follow the musical key for the book.*)

The next cáscara patterns conform to 2-3 (reverse) direction of the clave. It is the way that Changuito feels more comfortable playing. You can and should learn the patterns in the 3-2 (forward) direction of the clave.

Listen to the accent in the cáscara. This accent pattern goes back many years as was testified to by Cheverongo (Elpidio Serra Fundora). Cheverongo is a retired percussionist, well into his 70s and living in Havana. My interview with Cheverongo was exciting; the man has lived through many of the changes in Cuban popular music. Meeting him was an honor. Imagine meeting this frail-looking older man in a pork-pie hat and one of the first things he asks you to do is "play danzón for me." He wanted to know if I knew about Cuban music. He listened to me then sat right down on the floor, with these two funky drumsticks, and played a beautiful danzón on the concrete. I then proceeded to ask questions about timbales and we inevitably got around to the cáscara. Transcribed for you is the pattern which Cheverongo played as cáscara. Notice that the right hand plays only the accented notes. Cheverongo said that he was playing this pattern in the '40s. This method of playing the cáscara is distinctively Afro-Cuban and is most important when regarding feel and swing.

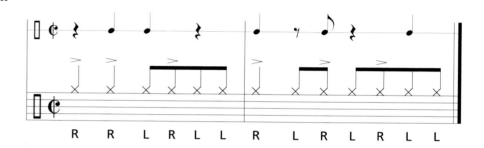

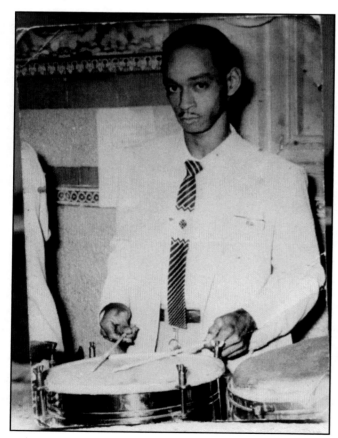

Cheverongo then…

…and now

Accenting the Cáscara Pattern

On the accompanying CD you will hear Changuito playing the cáscara pattern with and without conga accompaniment. In this way you can hear how the conga and timbales work together and also you can hear the timbales alone.

Here is the cáscara with no accompaniment in the hembra. Notice the accent pattern. This is a very important part of the cáscara pattern. This particular cáscara pattern is in 2-3 (reverse) clave direction.

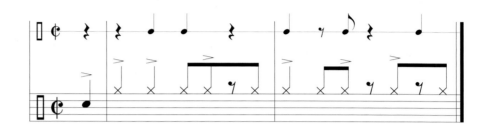

Changuito has a particular, favorite way of playing the closed and open tones in the hembra. Example two shows that pattern. Notice where the open tone plays, on the 4th eighth note of each measure and closes on the 7th eighth note. This gives a certain swing to the mixture of conga tumbao and hembra sobado. Very importantly, Changuito holds the timbale stick in his left hand while

playing the open and closed tones. This occurs in many of these patterns. Changuito sometimes plays a "deadened note with finger" on the hembra on the 2nd note of each measure. This is a natural movement for the hands, and gives a continuity to the movement. This has not been transcribed but you may want to try it once the transcribed exercise has been mastered.

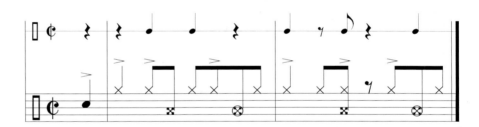

Here is a more typical approach to the closed and open sounds in the hembra. The open sound now compliments the conga and bass tumba. (There is no bass on the recording,

but very typically speaking, there would more often than not be a bass note either on the fourth quarter note of the measure or the bass pattern would emphasize this note.)

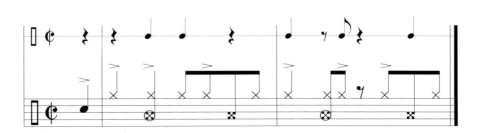

The cáscara in 3-2 (forward) direction. First just the pattern played on the shell.

4.

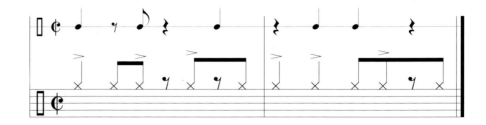

Adding one of Changuito's favorite hembra patterns

5.

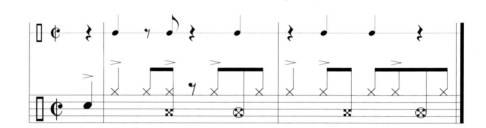

Once again, doubling the tumbao of the conga provides a very different sound and feel. This accompaniment seems to strength-en the tumbao whereas the other pattern, by offsetting the tumbao, gives the groove a very different feel.

6.

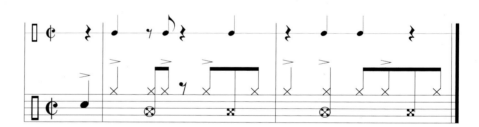

Here is a 16-measure phrase with cáscara, using both open/close patterns in the hembra. It's a good chance for you to hear the difference in texture created by each pattern, without the congas.

7.

The cáscara is rooted in the clave. The clave is the backbone of much, if not all, of Afro-Cuban popular music. The direction of the clave, whether 2-3 (reverse clave direction) or 3-2 (forward clave direction) has everything to do with the feel of the particular song or part of the music. (Due to composer/arranger discretion, the way in which a piece of music is arranged may reflect a "change" in the direction of the clave. This change will then affect the feel of different sections of the arrangement.)

These examples show the playing of the cáscara and clave together. This is not a simple exercise. First you must be able to feel the cáscara pattern. Here are two suggestion for practicing this pattern:

1) First play the cáscara, in one hand, without accents while the other hand rests. Add the clave in the other hand one note at a time, after repeating each small phrase many times. When you can play the whole pattern, add the accents, one at a time, until you are playing the whole two-handed pattern.

2) Try performing the exercise with both hands, starting with very short phrases of a few eighth notes each. Here is a step-by-step approach to playing the cáscara pattern and clave. This particular approach is written with the 2-3 direction of the son and rumba claves in mind. Of course, it can be used for the 3-2 direction of both son and rumba clave.

This is a basic building block exercise with five parts. The key is to proceed to the next level once you have developed a feel for the level on which you are working. Start with very short phrases of a few eighth notes each. Exercise 1 is the "2" part of the clave phrase.

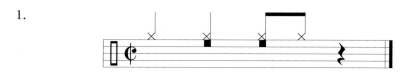

1.

Exercise 2 adds a few more notes and rests, resulting in a bit more of the phrase.

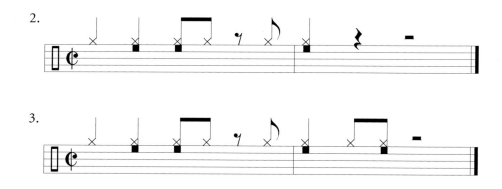

2.

3.

Exercise 4 is the whole cáscara/clave combination, 2-3 direction.

4.

Exercise 5 is the "3" part of the rumba clave. Substitute this in the previous exercise for the rumba clave in 2-3 direction.

5.

This technique also can be used when practicing with the accents in the cáscara pattern.

Examples of Cáscara and Clave

1.

Listen to the CD for this pattern with congas.

2.

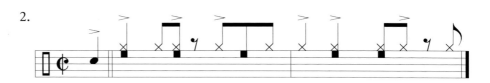

Listen to the CD for this pattern with congas.

Cáscara and Rumba Clave

Rumba clave is another distinct clave with its own feel and applications. Whereas, in older Afro-Cuban popular songs, the rumba clave was not a very common phrase to be heard, in the '80s and '90s with Cuban groups like Los Van Van, Irakere, NG La Banda, Charanga Habanera, and other great groups, the rumba clave is being heard in popular dance music more and more. It gives the music a different swing with its more syncopated rhythm. The change between rumba clave and son clave is only one note, but, oh, what that one note can do!

Here is the cáscara pattern with rumba clave in the 2-3 direction. Listen to the CD for this pattern with congas.

1.

Listen to the CD for this pattern with congas.

Here is the cáscara pattern with rumba clave in 3-2 direction.

2.
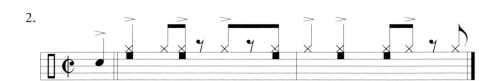

Listen to the CD for this pattern with congas.

When you can play these cáscara and clave patterns well, you will be able to better experience the difference in feel afforded by each phrase.

Two-Handed Cáscara Patterns

The cáscara pattern can also be played with each hand playing on the corresponding shell of the timbales. (Amadito Valdés tells us that this pattern is used when the tempo is slow.) New styles are constantly in development and so it is with this method of playing cáscara. Rather than the left hand just filling in when the right hand does not play, certain embellishments have been added to spice up the groove. Here are three examples of this style.

1.

R L R L R R L R   R L R R L R L R L   R L R L R L R L R   R L R R L R L R

Adding the congas (on the CD) you can hear how the two parts interact.

2.

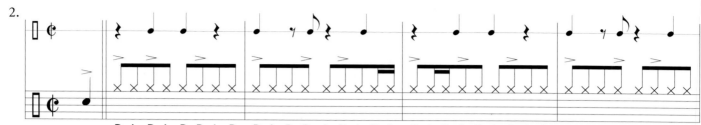

R L R L R R L R   R L L R R   L R L R L   R L R L R L R L R   R L R R   L R L R

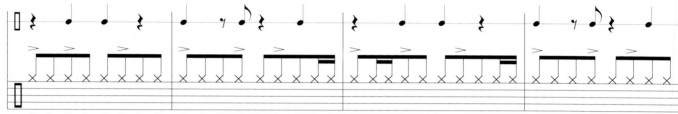

R L R L R R L R   R L R R   L R L R L   R L R L R L R L R L   R L R R   L R L R

R L R L R R L R   R L R R   L R L R L R L   R L R L R L R L R   R L R R   L R L R

R L R L R R L R   R L R R   L R L R L R L   R L R L R L R L R   R L R R   L R L R

This cáscara groove has some tricky sticking but you'll notice that the important accent pattern is maintained throughout.

3.

R L R L R R L R L R L   R L R R   L R L R L   R L R L R L R L R L   R L R R   L R L R

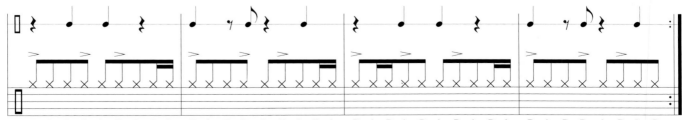

R L R R L R L R L   R L R R   L R L R L   R L R L R L R L R L R L   R L R R   L R L R

Mambo~The Cáscara **53**

Adding the Bass Drum

The bass drum can be used in many different ways with timbales. Using a bass drum is not at all a prerequisite to playing timbales. It just adds to the tonal possibilities and may add some extra punch. One common use is to help to punctuate cymbal crashes. Changuito uses the bass drum as part of the overall groove, whether during verses or bridges, he uses it as mentioned, to accentuate certain musical passages, and he uses it, very sparingly, during his solos. This first example with the bass drum is a relatively simple one; adding the bass drum to the down beat of every other measure in the cáscara groove.

1.

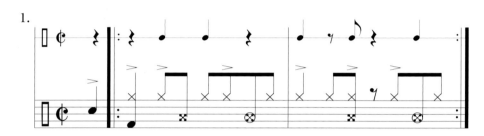

With this next musical example, the bass drum takes the place of an open hembra in the "3" part of the clave. (The "open hembra" is from Changuito's favorite hembra pattern.) You'll notice that the groove, in those measures, is maintained by a closed sound, with the finger, on the hembra. In this way there is a continuity of musical motion, enhancing the swing and feel.

2.

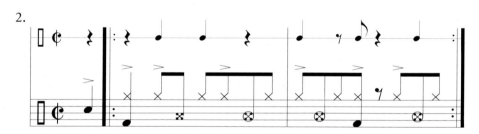

Here is a simple pattern for bass drum while playing the cáscara pattern. Take note of the accents in the cáscara. The bass drum is not overstated in this pattern. It plays a supportive, not an overpowering, role.

3.

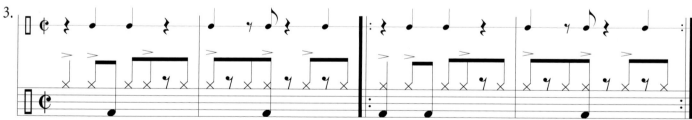

Amadito Valdés, a great timbalero residing in Havana, has some wonderful ideas about playing the cáscara. Presented is just one. (You will not find this on the CD.) Amadito uses the closed tone, played with the fingers of the hand, in an interesting way.

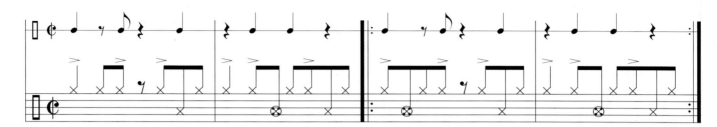

The Abanico within the Mambo

We have already discussed the roots and role of the abanico in the section on chachachá. The role of the abanico in the mambo is similar in that it is used to introduce a new section of the song being played. Very typically, the abanico has been used to introduce the section of a song featuring the coro (chorus). This is by no means a hard and fast rule as is demonstrated by Changuito and other musicians.

The abanico, when begun on the "3" part of the clave, has its first strong accent on the second clave beat in that measure. Changuito calls this abanico "abanico a contratiempo" because it begins on a syncopated part of the measure, the "and" of "2."

Compact Disc 32 Track

Compact Disc 33 Track

1.

Adding the 7 stroke roll in the abanico.

2.

R   L L R R L L   R

Adding the Mambo Bell

After playing the cáscara and then abanico it has been customary for the timbalero to switch from the cáscara pattern to bell. Since there is an accent in the macho (smaller drum) on the downbeat of the abanico, following the 7 stroke roll, the bell pattern as written must start on the quarter note following the downbeat or beginning of the measure. Here is an exercise to get you used to this transition. One thing to notice are the subtle accents in the campana. These, as with the accents in the cáscara, are important for overall feel. These subtly accented notes really lock in the groove. A crescendo marking shows you how the bell pattern is to be played. You can really hear how this feels by listening to the CD.

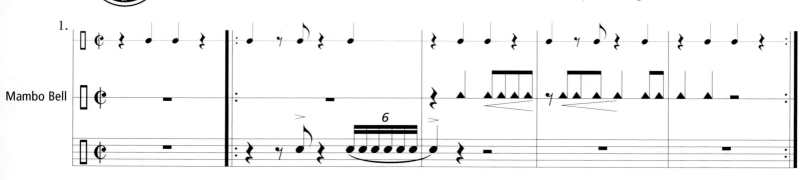

Mambo Bell

Adding one of the patterns for the hembra. It's not overemphasizing to say that these patterns in the hembra, even though not very loud in comparison to other instruments, are nevertheless very important. They help to tie all the instruments together in a unifying groove.

Mambo Bell

Here is another pattern for the hembra. (Notice that in measure 15 Changuito throws in one of his special "surprises"!)

3.

Mambo Bell

Adding the wood block playing clave is an important pattern to learn. Here is the bell pattern, preceded by the abanico, with the 2-3 son clave.

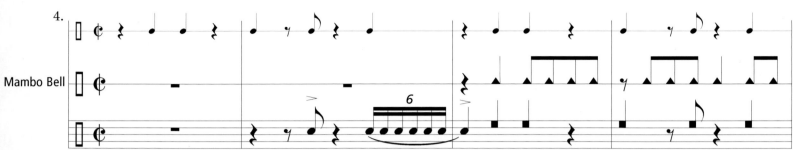

Mambo Bell

Now listen to the CD for this pattern with congas.

Changuito is a veritable treasure trove of great percussion ideas and he certainly is not at a loss for ideas when it comes to bell patterns. Presented are 2 ideas pertaining to these patterns. They are advanced patterns. Relatively easy to read, they really say a lot about tension and release and feel. The open and closed tones in the hembra are maintained while the bell pattern is pushed and pulled, time-wise, throughout the measures. Listen to the way the bell pattern is phrased, using the accented notes to push the beat while phrasing within the framework of the measure to create the tension and release necessary for the pattern's movement.

A note: please make sure that you can play, and play well, the patterns already out-

lined. The bell pattern from the previous exercises is one of the most common for this style of Afro-Cuban popular music. You must be able to feel this pattern before proceeding on.

The pattern in the hembra is also not to be overlooked. There is a fair amount of independence work occurring within this pattern. Use methods already outlined to achieve the optimum performance of these patterns.

And lastly, listen to the subtle crescendo in the bell during certain sections of the pattern. This is yet another way to make the pattern groove more, swing more, and make the music really sing. You need to approximate all of these variables as closely as possible.

Mambo Bell

Now with the other open and closed pattern in the hembra.

6.

Mambo Bell

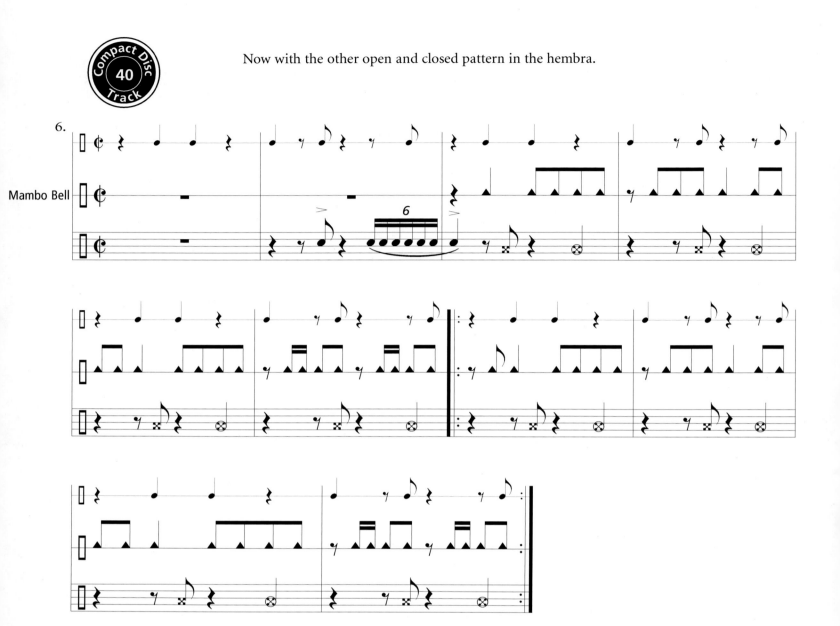

Combining the Mambo and Bongo Bells

The role of the timbalero has constantly been changing and adapting. As early as the 1970s Changuito was defying barriers and stretching the role of the timbalero. He was making inroads for more creativity, creating a greater role as musician and not just as time-keeper, and constantly developing new methods of playing. One of the important playing techniques developed by Changuito was the ability to play two bell parts simultaneously. These two bell parts were the "normal" part of the timbalero, played on what many musicians call the "mambo bell," along with the bell part played by the bongocero

(bongo player), called, by some, the "bongo bell." This bongo bell part is most important because, in many cases, it states the down-beat while other rhythms play off of it. The sound of the bongo bell is strong and constant. It provides the downbeats off of which the other syncopated rhythms can really work. The bongo bell part is one of the cornerstones upon which much of the groove depends. The other, and most important, is of course clave.

Here is the bongo bell part in the 2-3 clave direction.

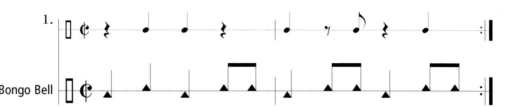

The mambo bell part is traditionally played by the timbalero during choruses and other sections of mambo style songs. Here is one of the most typical of mambo bell patterns. It is played, in this case, in the 2-3 clave direction.

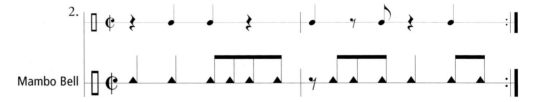

Playing the two parts together is an increasingly typical way of playing timbales. When would you want to use this technique? The obvious time to use this is when there is no bongocero in the musical group with which you are playing. What this pattern does is provide a typical, full sounding pattern complete with a pattern rooted in downbeats (bongo bell), a most typical syncopated rhythm, all with the clave as the backbone. Of course, there are some inherent problems with this pattern. You will need to work on the independence. This can be done in several different ways, as noted before.

Play both patterns, slowly, a small phrase at a time, adding a note or two only after the previous phrase has been mastered.

Play one pattern, slowly, and add the other pattern one note at a time until both phrases are unified in the groove.

Changuito has another important and exciting method for developing independence. Play one pattern and sing the other pattern. This will assist you greatly in learning to perform both together. Most probably, this method develops a different part of your independence vocabulary, and it assists your actual performance. Try it. It definitely helps to "internalize" the rhythms. As a matter of fact, try singing all the parts we have been practicing: clave, cáscara, campana, bongo bell. Perhaps you will become more intimate with the rhythms, helping you to better feel and utilize them in your playing.

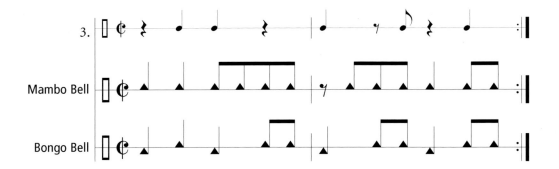

Adding the Bass Drum

The bass drum can add some extra rhythmic excitement to this groove. It can also add another level of independence work. The important thing to know is that this mode of performing is typical regarding Changuito. It is an integral part of his playing and definitely gives his grooves their distinctive feel.

Notice the placement of the bass drum. Its syncopation serves to propel the beat, not bog it down. If the bass drum was copying exactly what the bassist might play (i.e. "and of 2 and 4") there may be a tendency to weigh the groove down. This syncopated pattern spices the groove just right.

Ahh, Changuito and his mambo bell patterns! Although we have studied this pattern before, the addition of the bass drum and bongo bell really make this pattern feel great. Remember: practice slowly and methodically. When you feel comfortable with any of these patterns, either try them with a rhythm section or break out your favorite Los Van Van CDs and play along! Either way you'll find out soon enough if you've got timba! (Timba is a Cuban slang for groove or swing.)

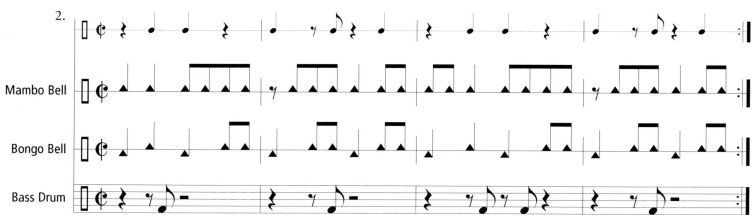

Amadito Valdes has a pattern using two bells that should be learned.

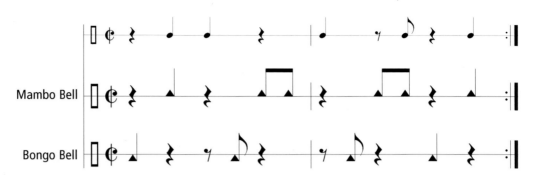

Mambo Bell

Bongo Bell

Please do keep in mind that most of the tempos on the accompanying CD are relatively slow, for listening and learning ease. It is important that you learn these rhythms and combinations at these slow (and slower) tempos. It is the best and most advantageous way to learn. But different tempos will provide different feels, so once you have these rhythms "under your belt," play them at different tempos to achieve the different rhythmic "movements." (One of the many ways which Changuito describes these grooves is with the Spanish word "movimiento" or "movement.")

The Intro Fill

This fill idea is a very common "lick" commonly used as the introduction to many Afro-Cuban style popular songs. The open tone on the hembra is not struck excessively. Just enough to get the open tone. The most important part is the combination of the accented macho and the open tone in the hembra.

Making transitions, starting from silence and moving into a groove, then making a transition to another groove, is what all musicians are constantly doing. Beginning a song, going from intro to verse, verse to chorus, chorus back to verse, this is something that you, a timbalero, must be accustomed to doing. On the accompanying CD tracks for this section you will hear Changuito playing patterns we already have transcribed in this book. This is the reason why certain parts of this exercise are not transcribed. Throughout the book you will find information that "fits" in this exercise.

The "Intro Fill" is followed by a verse section where you will hear the cáscara with bombo (bass drum). Then you will hear what Changuito calls "una preparación," a prepara-

tion. There are four of these "preparaciones." Enjoy them! Each "preparación" is two measures long, corresponding to the clave. After each, Changuito plays what he would normally play for a chorus section corresponding to the style in which he is playing: two bells and bass drum. You will then hear the transition fill ("Intro Fill") again and then we go back down to the cáscara pattern for the verse. This is repeated several times.

This exercise is very important. There are many patterns you can use to "fill in" the verse and chorus sections of the Transition Exercise. The most important concept behind developing this brief but significant exercise is that it all must "flow." It must swing. You must be sure of what you are playing. The dancers are depending on you!

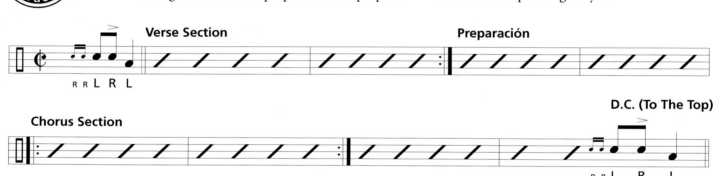

PILÓN

Pilón is a rhythm invented by Enrique Bonne in the Oriente province of Cuba. Pacho Alonso made the pilón famous with his group, Los Bocucos. The dance of the pilón imitates the motion one makes when grinding coffee. "Pilón" is Spanish for "pestle," the vessel that you grind things in.

Ritmo pilón refers to a way of dancing to the son style. It's done by placing the hands in front of you, in a closed fist, one atop the other and making a stirring motion.

Changuito has developed the pilón into an art form. Presented are some of his ideas.

Preliminary Exercises

Exercise 1 features going from the chacha bell to the accented macho with the right hand.

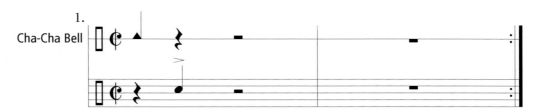

Adding the open hembra, played with the left stick. Also, you will be playing a cross-stick with the left hand.

There are a few movements you will be making with both hands, so take it slow.

Exercise 3 features open tones on the hembra, played with the left stick, accompanied by chacha bell played with the right hand.

Once again, there are several movements you are making with both hands.

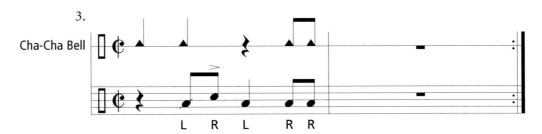

We will build the pilón in sections, first starting with bell and cross-stick. This is a very basic beginning, but you are still advised to take it slow.

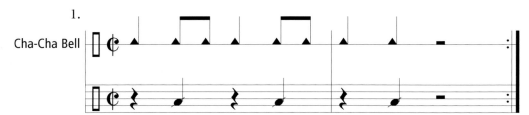

Adding the macho (high drum) and hembra (low drum), we start to see and feel the independence required to play this pattern. The hand playing the bell (right handed players should play the bell with right hand) will now also play the macho. The hand playing the cross stick on the hembra will now also play the hembra open tone with stick. Take it slow! It's not easy to go from bell to a very positive rim shot on the macho. Just practicing going from bell to rim shot is a very good idea. Do that a few hundred times. Make sure the height of the timbales allows this very basic movement. The same thing goes with the hembra cross-stick to the hembra open tone. These have to be very natural movements in order for the full groove to do just that, groove and make sense musically.

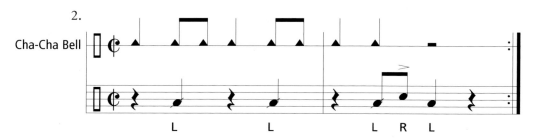

A bit more of the pattern is revealed with two more notes in the hembra and bell. This two-bar pattern is performed 4 separate times on the CD. One of the reasons this was done was to give you a chance to rest before having to "think" about playing the pattern again. Play it one time through then take a break. Jump into it again. Notice where it feels good. Notice where there are little "hitches" in the pattern where you do not feel comfortable. Take some time to work on these sections of this two-bar groove before attempting to play it for longer periods of time.

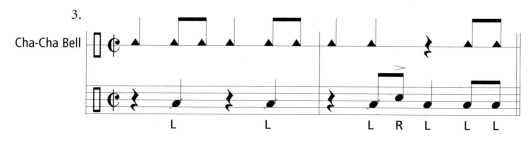

This is a "complete" pilón groove.

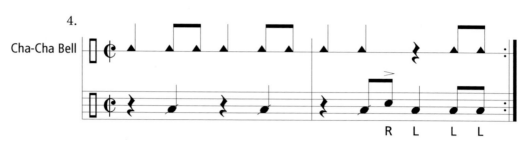

A bit more advanced, this groove will once again call on your relaxed, controlled independence and groove. Changuito plays the three-bar phrase three times. Practice this short phrase slowly and carefully. Take your time and take a break in between each phrase to examine what may have been uncomfortable areas within the groove.

Here are some areas to think about:
- *How did the mix of hembra and bell feel?*
- *The transition from bell to macho?*
- *Overall time feel throughout the phrase?*
- *Transition from cross stick to open tone in the hembra?*

Now the pilón, advanced pattern.

Cha-Cha Bell

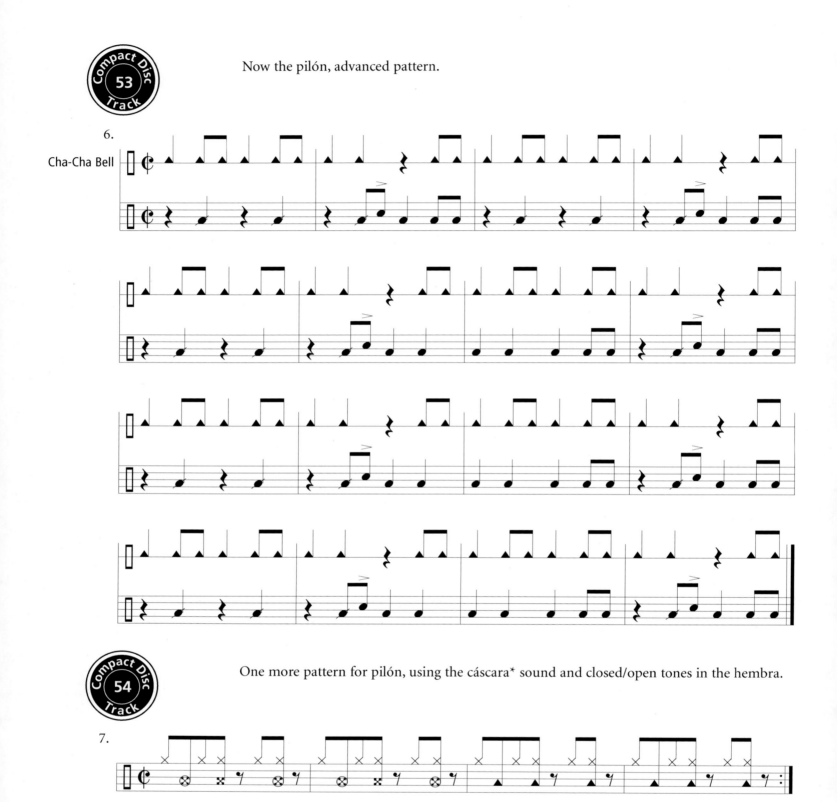

One more pattern for pilón, using the cáscara* sound and closed/open tones in the hembra.

*This refers to the sound of the cáscara or shell, **not** the cáscara pattern.

MOZAMBIQUE

The famous Cuban musician Pello el Afrokán (Pedro Izquierdo) invented mozambique. There are many stories as to how or why this rhythm was invented. Many people believe the "how" is that the mozambique rhythm is a derivation of the conga combined with elements of rumba. (Rumba is an Afro-Cuban rhythmic tradition.)

An important essence of the Mozambique is that of a brass band with many drummers. Typically, you can find 10 congeros and a full section of trombones making up the mozambique. The rhythm is a mixture of comparsa, rumba, and this "brass band." According to Dr. Olavo Alén Rodriguez, mozambique was quite popular after its invention in the early '60s.

Preliminary Exercises

Let's concentrate on the mouth and body of the mambo bell. This first exercise is the first measure of the Mozambique rhythm.

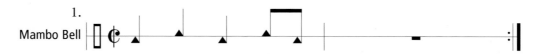

Here is the second measure:

Pay close attention to the next exercises on the CD. They will introduce you to the combinations of bell (mouth and body), open hembra with stick, and muffled hembra with stick.

We will look at playing the bombo and clave for mozambique later in this chapter. Here are some ideas for getting started with this section. First, the chacha bell and open hembra with stick.

Add the hembra muffled with the stick. Muffling the sound of the hembra after playing the drum "open" (with the stick) requires

touch and taste. Take your time. As with all of the exercises to get you accustomed to specific rhythms, take it slow and relaxed.

A combination of chacha bell and open and muffled hembra with stick.

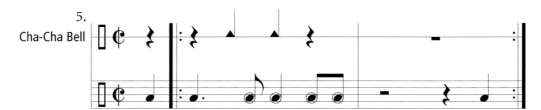

Primary Bell Patterns

One of the many great features of the mozambique are the bell patterns. Here is a primary pattern which Changuito plays on the mambo bell, utilizing the mouth and body of the bell for two distinct sounds. At first it might be a good idea for you to pick up the bell and play it. This gives you a more intimate feel with the bell. You can feel how it resonates in your hand; how the open tone resonates more than the tone from the body of the bell. This pattern does not necessarily have to be played on a mambo bell. A smaller bell (cha bell) or different bell (bongo bell) can work also.

The most important parts of this pattern are:
• the actual rhythm you are playing
• the feel of the rhythm (once you understand the pattern)
• the sounds of the bell.

Once you have spent some time with this, mount the bell on your timbales and get the same feeling that you had while holding the bell.

The rumba clave accompanies this pattern. Here is the primary bell pattern for mozambique.

And now, adding the hembra with the mozambique bell pattern. The next three exercises build the pattern of bell and hembra. The three gradually add the hembra, both closed and open tones, along with the mozambique bell pattern. The most important thing to remember is that this pattern really swings when all the parts are synchronized. Keep that

in mind as you slowly proceed through these levels. (Slowly repeat after me: I know it will groove, I know it will groove...)

A refresher note about practicing. Listen to what you are playing. Watch what you are playing. Feel for the spots and sources of tension.

2b.

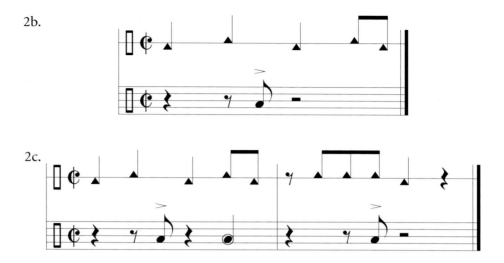

2c.

This is the full mozambique pattern for timbales. When you have successfully performed Levels 2a-2c, you're ready for the whole pattern. What has been added to finish the pattern is the fourth quarter note of the second measure which now has two eighth notes on the bell (body) and a closed note in the hembra (played with the stick). Slowly, carefully, with respect for the tradition-that's the way to practice this. Then break out some records and play along!

3.

Mambo Bell

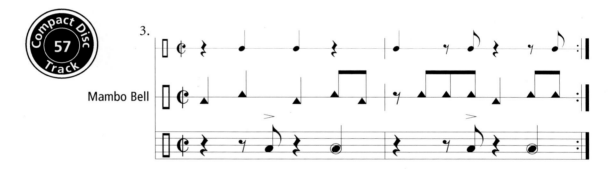

Mozambique Bell and Rumba Clave

Here is another pattern which works well and grooves hard. Playing rumba clave in one hand and the mozambique bell pattern involves some independence. But learning this pattern is well worth the effort. You can approach this pattern the same way as we did the bell-hembra combination. Take the pattern one small step at a time until you have the full phrase grooving. Although this pattern begins on the "2" part of the mozambique bell pattern, Changuito insists that one should begin playing the clave on the "3" part. He is adamant that you would never start the clave on the "2" part.

Mambo Bell

Clave and Bombo (bass drum)

In mozambique, this bombo, or bass drum part, is a typical pattern. (The bass drum is not your typical bass drum, played with the foot. It is a drum played with a stick and is strapped to the player much like a military style bass drum.) Now we are really getting into some serious independence work. One hand is playing rumba clave on the body of the chacha bell. The other is playing the bombo part. You know the drill by now. Take your time and refer to the section of the book, How to Practice, for assistance. Also, please pay particular attention to how

Changuito phrases this, and many other musical phrases throughout this book. Quoting ethnomusicologist Weihua Zhang from China, "Part of the beauty and rhythmic tension of African, African-American, and other world music is the conscious blurring of durational values between duple and triple..." Changuito, as well as many other Afro-Cuban percussionists, is a master of this idiom. It's not a technique. It's a way of life and of musical expression. Try your best to understand and then emulate this phrasing. It is part and parcel of the Afro-Cuban feel.

Another bombo pattern opposite the rumba clave. Difficult? Yes. Worth it? Definitely!

MERENSONGO

T his rhythm was invented by Changuito and is a mixture of merengue from the Dominican Republic and songo.

Changuito has used merensongo with Los Van Van and is constantly finding new applications for it.

Preliminary Exercises

Here is an exercise for mouth and body of the mambo bell with muffled hembra played with the stick. The rhythm in the mambo bell is different from mozambique.

Four sounds necessary for proper execution of merensongo make up this exercise.

The open hembra is featured in these excerpts.

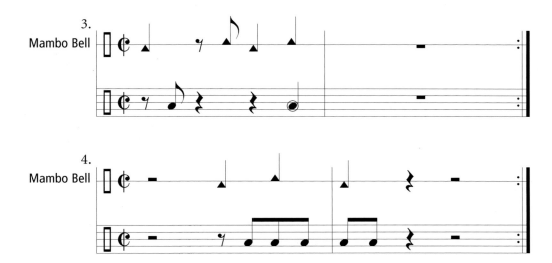

Basic Merensongo

As you can see, you will be playing the mambo bell, mouth (open sound) and body for this pattern. Here is the basic bell pattern.

More Advanced Merensongo

The next, more advanced, level of meren-songo adds a bit more in the hembra. Even though this rhythm is not a recent invention of Changuito, the percussionists and drum set artists in Cuba use it in very modern popular dance music. You can hear the influence of this next "level" of the rhythm, where the five open tones are added in the hembra.

This level requires a lot of study. You should know by now how to take apart the measures of the groove, dividing them into their least common independence denominators. What this means is finding the small-

est fraction of the groove where you may have problems with the independence. Start from there. Do not leave there until you can perform, with feeling, this individual part of the overall groove.

Please note, when listening to the CD, that the five consecutive open tones have a crescendo feel, culminating in a slight accent on the fifth note. By "crescendo feel" I mean that it is not an actual crescendo, per se, but the resultant feel provides a very big part of the overall groove.

Adding the Bass Drum~Preliminary Exercises

Here are three building block exercises to help you develop the independence and feel necessary to play the next example.

Merensongo With Bass Drum Added

And now we will add the bass drum to the "basic" and "next" levels of mérengsongo. Even though there is only one bass drum note added to each measure, it really helps to add to the rhythmic excitement and movement.

This next example is probably the most intense rhythmic activity we've examined so far. Each two-bar pattern changes either slightly or dramatically in its note content. But the feel never varies. You could, and possibly should, practice each two-bar pattern separately, concentrating on the technical aspects of independence and correct placement of stick on playing surface (i.e. playing from the mouth to the body of the bell(s) where notated), while the other limb is playing its part on another surface. Note the ghosted notes, especially in the second measure of each phrase. Though

there are not many, they never interfere with the flow of the groove, but instead subtly add the necessary spice and shading to propel the groove along.

Yes, our suggestion is to take each two-bar pattern and practice it until it becomes part of your repertoire. Then and only then progress to the next two measures. When four measures can be played proceed to the next two, and so on. Here are five building block exercises, not included on the CD, which will help you develop the bell, hembra, and bass drum pattern.

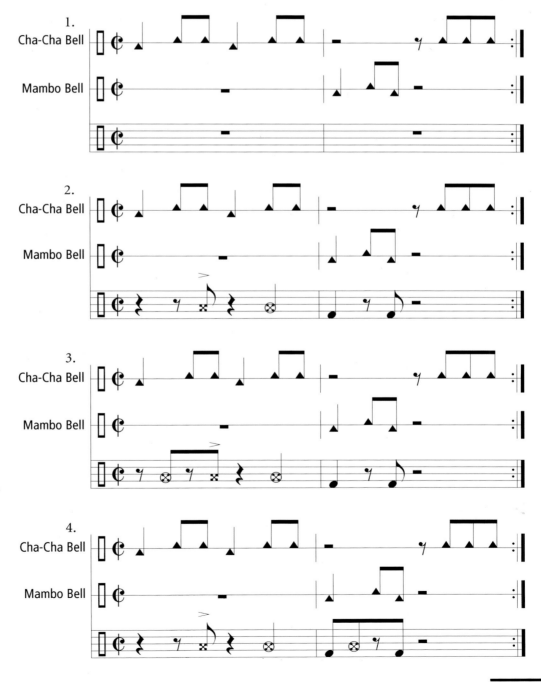

Merensongo~Another Variation

And here is the full pattern.

Advanced Merensongo~Preliminary Exercises

Here are six building block exercises, not included on the CD, which will help you develop the bell, hembra, and bass drum pattern for the next example.

Merensongo~Advanced Pattern

Another pattern for merensongo, this time with a new bell pattern, the open tones in the hembra, and bass drum. Definitely advanced and most definitely worth the effort.

Cha-Cha Bell

CONGA

Conga is a rhythm typically used during carnaval in Cuba. The group which plays conga is called comparsa. (This group is relatively like the samba schools in Brasil.) The drums used for conga are similar throughout the island, except in Santiago de Cuba where the comparsas use bocú, a cone-shaped drum.

Conga Habanera is related to rhumba. It uses tumbadoras, three in total. The tumbadoras are slung around the neck of the drummers during the carnaval parade. The drums used by the comparsa are requinto, quinto, tumbas or congas. These drums harken back to the African heritage of drums from Dahomey and from the bantú. The bass drums used for conga are : bombo (approximate size: 10"x26"), pilandera (smaller bass drum, 10"x24" or 10"x20") and galleta (smallest bass drum, 4" to 6" inches by 20".) Sartenes (Spanish for "frying pans") are fastened in pairs to holders which can be then worn by participants in the comparsa. Hand bells and snare drums are also used.

El batutero, the leader of the ensemble, is like a "drum major" complete with the "baton," gives the calls with the whistle. These "calls" are for breaks in the rhythm, turns and steps by the dancers, among many other things.

Conga Oriental comes from the eastern provinces of Cuba, the Oriente provinces. In Santiago de Cuba, the comparsa uses, instead of frying pans, brake drums. The guataca, or hoe blade, is also used. Atcheres or maracas are also used within the comparsa. In Havana, trumpet or cornet is used in the comparsa but in the Oriente region of Cuba the corneta china or trompeta china, a double-reeded instrument of the oboe family, is used. This instrument has a very characteristic piercing sound which is utilized to penetrate the massive sound of the percussion. Everyone in the comparsa, playing the rhythm of conga, plays some type of percussion instrument. Conga habanera is more like urban music, while conga oriental is more rural in nature.

Preliminary Exercises

Changuito's method of performing the conga also utilizes the mambo bell and muffled/open sounds in the hembra. The bell pattern is different than mozambique or pilón. Here is a look at one measure of conga. You will be playing 4 sounds.

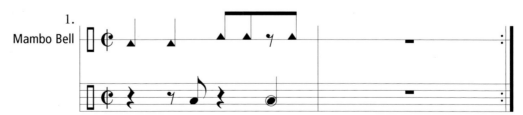

Another measure of a basic conga.

Utilizing the chacha and mambo bells for conga provides interesting challenges and great grooves. We must accustom ourselves to playing on two surfaces (the two bells), while two sounds from bell and body are played on the mambo bell.

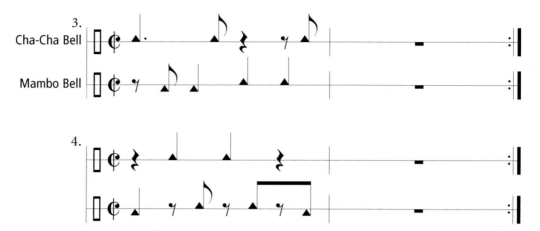

Adding the bass drum and open tone in the hembra, play with the hand which is playing clave. (Changuito plays clave with his left hand.)

Basic Bell Pattern

As with many of the rhythms we have been studying, the bell pattern plays an important role in conga. The clave has been added so you can feel this most important relationship.

Adding the hembra provides some of the real feel for conga habanera. Once again the clave is played and written for you to feel and understand the meaningful connection between rhythm and "key."

2.

Mambo Bell

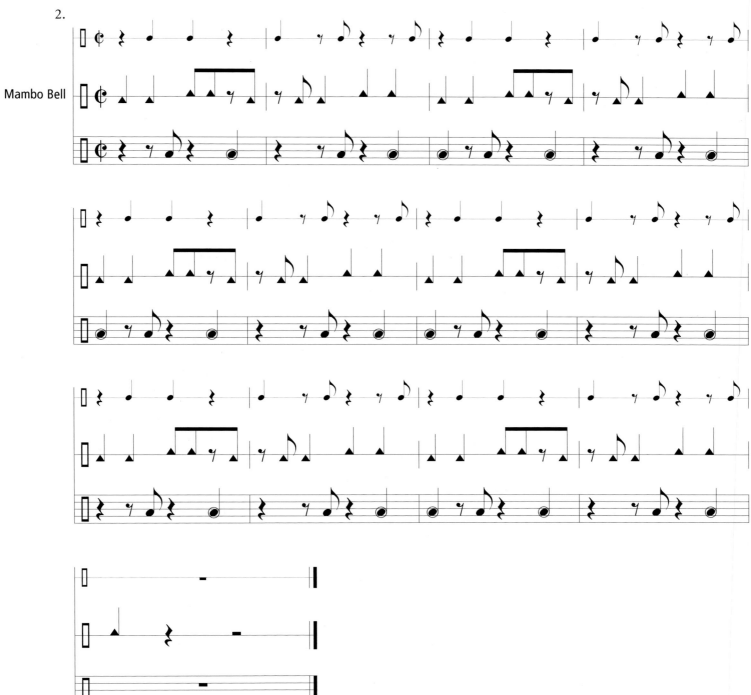

Adding the Bass Drum

The addition of the bass drum adds both a bottom end and an "anchor" to the conga groove. It also adds one more level of inde-pendence work. If you have worked through the previous exercises you should not have a problem with this pattern.

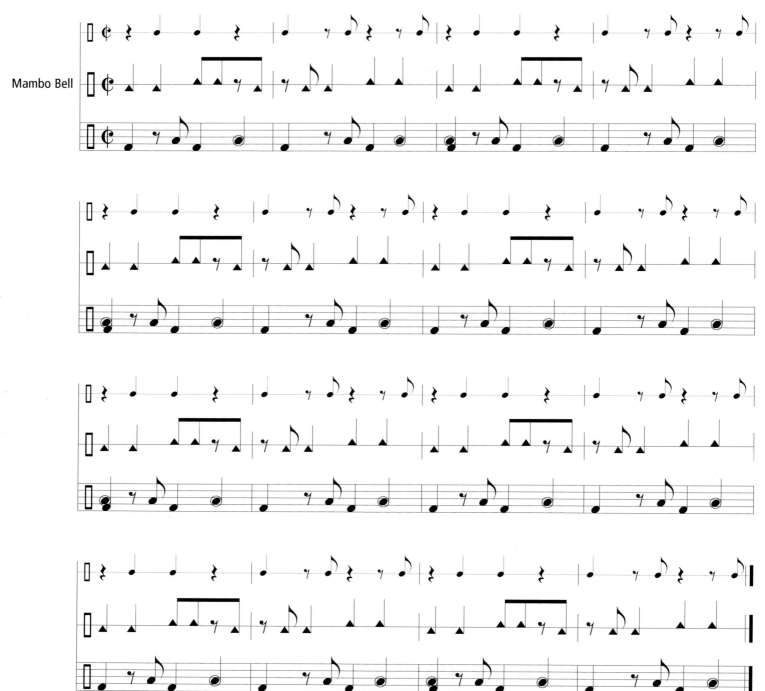

Mambo Bell

Another Bell Pattern for the Conga Habanera

1.

Add the clave to the preceding bell pattern. The clave is played, in this example, on the chacha bell. (You will notice, as in other examples in the book, the bells have been written in a different manner in the staff. This is done for ease of reading.) This pattern and its groove are well worth the time you will spend learning it.

2.

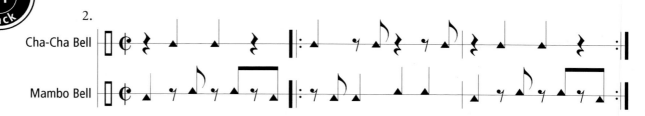

Adding the Bass Drum

Adding the bass drum for that "anchored" groove and feeling, plus the open tone in the hembra. This is a great groove, with a very traditional feeling. We feel it's most important to learn this feeling.

⁶⁄₈ RHYTHMS

Changuito's mastery of 6/8 rhythms is legendary. This knowledge is now passed on to you. The roots of these rhythms come from Africa and Changuito has added new and exciting variations to these basic rhythms and patterns. Most importantly, they all feel and sound great. After some practice you will be able to approximate the sound of the CD and you'll be ready to apply this new knowledge to your own music.

Preliminary Exercises

Chacha bell and hembra, both open and muffled with fingers or hand, are featured in these 6/8 rhythm timbale applications.

⁶⁄₈ Bell Pattern

First, let's look at a very basic 6/8 bell rhythm, played for us on the chacha bell.

Next, we add the closed and open tones in the hembra. The first two measures are different from the remaining 14 and are basically timekeepers until the actual hembra pattern develops. The hembra pattern beginning with measures 7 and 8 and continuing until the end is an important pattern and should be considered the main "lesson" in this example.

2.

Cha-Cha Bell

Bembe Bell Pattern

Changuito calls this the "bembe" clave or pattern. Notice that the bell pattern is different than the previous 6/8 examples. You will also find some difficult patterns in the 4th, 8th, 12th, and 16th measures. As mentioned before, this pattern is an approximation of the playing in between triple and duple meter which is so common in many African-based types of music. It has been transcribed so as to be legible. There are several important patterns within this musical example. Measures 1 and 2 are very important. So are the aforementioned syncopated patterns. Listen to the CD and absorb the feel of the patterns. They are essential to Changuito as a player and to Cuban timbales, rhythm, and music.

Cha-Cha Bell

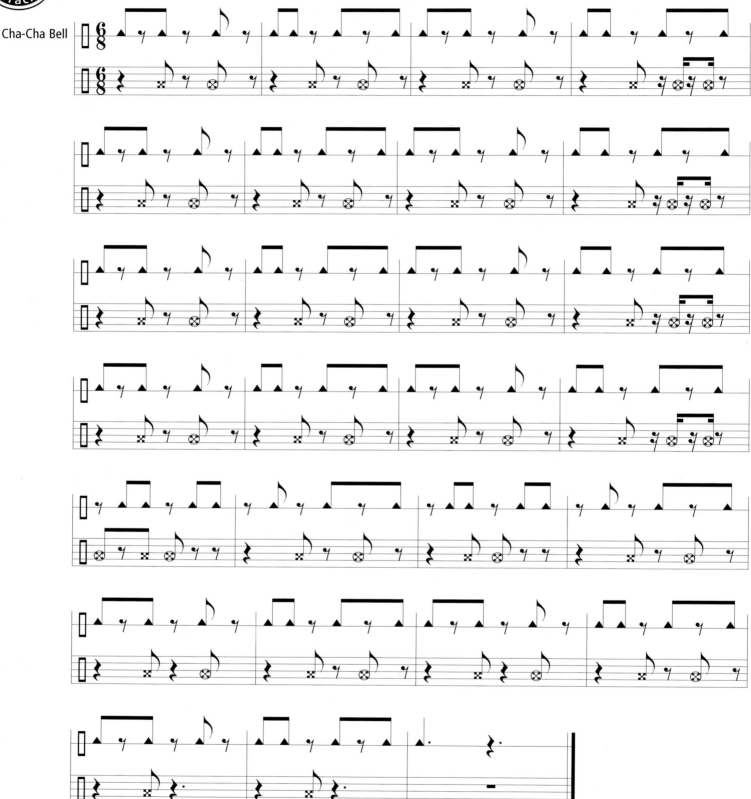

Another ⅛ Bell Pattern

This is another cowbell pattern Changuito uses for playing in ⅛.

Adding the open and closed tones in the hembra yields this result. All the practice techniques we have discussed in the book can be used here. Practice slowly, methodically, and with great care. You want to get as close as you can to the sound of the CD.

2.

Cha-Cha Bell

TIMBA SONGO LAYÉ

Changuito is a very inventive musician and this groove is one of his finest. Following are some preliminary exercises to help get you going with this groove. These exercises, as with all exercises found in the opening sections of each chapter, need to be practiced very slowly and carefully. Repeat each short phrase as many times as necessary to develop the technique for playing the pattern. This will insure the usefulness of the exercise.

Preliminary Exercises

Combine chacha bell, the sounds from both mouth and body of the bell, and cross stick in the hembra.

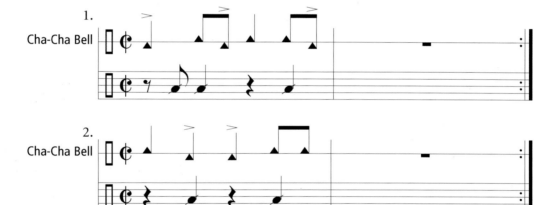

Add the open hembra, played with stick.

Another pattern using the open sound of the hembra.

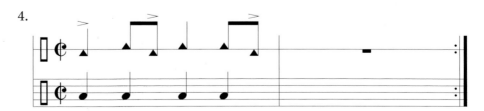

The Bell Pattern

Here is the bell pattern for this extremely funky rhythm. Note how the bell very clearly states the rumba clave. And, when you listen to the CD, please pay attention to how this pattern is phrased; pushing and pulling, all the tension/release creating a great groove.

The hand not playing bell plays cross stick on the hembra. Here is the pattern. The accent must remain in the bell while this pattern is being played in the hembra.

Adding an open sound in the hembra, played with the stick. The accent has become a bit less here, so we are using a staccato marking instead of an accent marking.

Another open tone pattern in the hembra gives this special groove another reason to swing! Measure 9 is special way of phrasing very typical to "afrocubanismo." Listen to the CD. Try and feel it for yourself. Imitate it because it is being played by a master.

4.
Cha-Cha Bell

Adding the bass drum provides yet another layer to this groove. The clave is not over-emphasized, so the staccato markings are used again. Measure 9, once again, is treated a bit differently. This time, though, it's a bit "straighter" then the previous example. It's written to reflect the subtle difference.

(By the way, both measure 9s in these two examples are not written correctly. This is just an approximation of the notation. Diagrams, symbols, and direction markings have been used by others to denote the "laid back" or "fast forward" movement in these phrases. In other words, listen to the CD!)

Compact Disc Track 82

5.

Cha-Cha Bell

INDEPENDENCE EXERCISES

How and why should we practice independence on timbales? We have all been taught, or wanted to learn at some point, the fine art of independence. It is a drumming trademark. This is a method, developed by Changuito, which is based on feel not notes, roots not exercise; playing cáscara, clave, 6/8 patterns, while soloing with the other limb. The solos are based on phrases that make beautiful musical sense. How to do it? You know the drill. Break the pattern down to their lowest common denominator, sticking patterns. Start slowly, one small increment at a time, until the whole phrase flows from your hands and heart. This section provides some very musical independence ideas which will assist you in developing your skills as a timbalero and percussionist.

Independence is a key ingredient in a drummer's ability to ably perform on his or her instrument. Changuito has developed this style into an amazing tour de force of percussion skill and musical mastery. Independence is one thing. This artistry combines the musical phrasing of disparate rhythms and rhythmic structures, molding them into a mind-boggling creative exploration. Anyone who has experienced this style of performance cannot help but be moved and challenged as a performer as well as a listener.

It is as performers that we must examine these phrases, first to develop a sense of the independence, then to delve deeper and work on the physical act. But when these are through, our goal is to play music, using the independence as a springboard from which to jump into waters charted by a few daring virtuosos. In Afro-Cuban music, Changuito is the captain of the crew.

Changuito uses these ideas as true solo ideas. In his many workshops around the world, Changuito at times performs as a solo percussionist. This is where these ideas come to life. They can work in a group setting but they shine when used in solos.

An idea from Changuito is to sing the solo line while playing the main rhythm, in these cases either cáscara or $\frac{6}{8}$ clave.

Cáscara in One Hand/ Solo Pattern in the Other Hand

(You may choose to do these musical exercises with either hand playing either part, further enhancing your independence.)

Changuito employs many different solo phrases in the left hand while the right hand plays cáscara on bell. Presented are several patterns, each of which will present unique challenges. (Please review "How to Practice this Book" for practice ideas.) Most important to the process is the phrasing. This can only be achieved after thorough practice of the technical aspects of the exercise. Take your time, go slowly, methodically, and you will eventually master these phrases and develop your own.

Independence Exercise 1

This first musical independence exercise is based on the relationship between the cáscara pattern in one hand and another syncopated, musical pattern in the other hand. We have broken down the pattern into small increments, making it easier to study and perform.

Pattern 1 features a short two-note phrase counterpoint to the cáscara pattern.

Pattern 2 extends the previous pattern by one note.

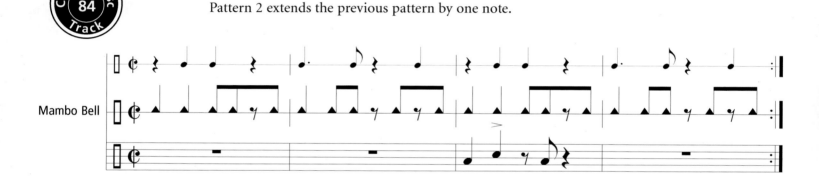

Pattern 3

Pattern 4 is played on the drums and is slowly making itself known. Play musically.

Pattern 5. Adding more to the pattern completes musical idea.

Pattern 6. Here is the the completed musical idea in its performance form.

Independence Exercise 2

This is another melodic independence "movement" featuring the cáscara pattern and a very syncopated, though logical, rhythmic accompaniment. This pattern is presented in a different, more flowing, manner than the previous group of musical examples. Perhaps this method will give you more of an insight as to the creative process involved in this idea.

Mambo Bell

Independence Exercise 3

Compact Disc Track 90

Changuito has developed some amazing musical ideas using his singularly extraordinary independence and musicality. Here is one phrase which demonstrates this amazing ability. Basically these are six-note phrases (beginning and ending with a rest), but the beauty should not be lost in the theory. There is a wonderful feeling imparted by this, and many other of Changuito's musical and inspiring phrases. Listen to the CD before you begin to read the example.

Independence Solo 1

All three of these musical ideas are now presented in a short independence solo showcase. Please notice, when listening to the CD, the seamlessness of the flow of ideas and the groove so inherent in the piece. Truly a work of art.

Mambo Bell

continues on next page

Mambo Bell

*continues on next page

Independence Solo 1 (continued)

Independence Ideas with the $\frac{6}{8}$ Clave or Bell Pattern

This first exercise demonstrates a relatively basic independence idea.

1.
Cha-Cha Bell

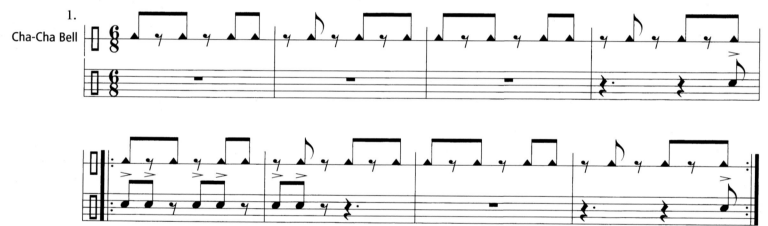

This second exercise is a bit more intense and melodic than the previous pattern.

continues on next page

Example 2 continued.

The third musical exercise. As with all exercises in this book, when listening to the CD pay particular attention to the phrasing. There are times when a literal transcription only comes close to what is actually being played. Attempting to transcribe certain phrases exactly would only serve to confuse rather than enlighten and educate. Listen to the CD for the best possible idea of how the notated rhythms are interpreted (felt).

Cha-Cha Bell

Independence Solo 2

And now, all three patterns played in a beautifully constructed solo. Please listen to the intensity and sure-handedness with which this solo is executed. The proper exe-cution of this solo would be a lofty goal for even the most seasoned of percussionists. Listen, listen, then listen some more. This is really a work of art.

continues on next page

Independence Solo 2 (continued)

*continues on next page

Changuito Solo Improvisation

REFERENCES

Los Instrumentos del la Musica Cubana
Fernando Ortiz
Direccion de Cultura, Ministerio de
Educación. La Habana, 1952, Volumes I, III, IV,
VII

Enciclopedia de Cuba
1955

Musica en el Folklore
Argeliers Leon

Los Timbales
Maria Elena Vinueza Gonzalez (1980)

Las Pailas Cubanas
Marta Rodriguez Cuervo

Las Pailas Cubanas
Melba Lucia Pascual Lopez (1988-9)

Approximación a las Pailitas Cubanas
Mireya Marti Reyes y Maxmiliana Jaquinet

La Música y el Pueblo
Maria Teresa Linares
Editorial Pueblo y Educación

De Lo Afro Cubano a la Salsa
Dr. Olave Alén Rodríguez
Ediciones ARTEX S.A.
La Habana, Cuba 1994

Percussioni (November 1991)
Interview with Tito Puente

El Mambo
Selección de Radamés Giro
Editorial Letras Cubanas
La Habana, Cuba 1993

*Miguel Faílde, creador musical del dan-
zón*
Osvaldo Castillo
CNC, La Habana 1964

Musica del Caribe
Jose Arteaga
Bogota, Colombia

Enciclopedia y Clasicos Cubanos
Natalio Galán Sariol
Madrid 1974

El Son Cubano - Antecedentes
Cristóbal Sosa López

La Clave Cubana
Cristóbal Sosa López

El Toque Latino
John Storm Roberts
ADAMEZ. Mexico 1982

*Nationalizing Blackness: "afrocubanismo"
and artistic revolution in Havana, 1920-
1940*
Robin Moore

LISTENING LIST

The following list of recordings and groups is compiled from the author's personal collection. Where no particular albums are listed, acquiring most of the work by the named artist would be very worthwhile.

Adalberto y su Son

Aragon, Orquesta

Aliamen, Orquesta

Barretto, Ray
Indestructible

Charanga Habanera, La

Delgado, Isaac

Fajardo, José
Cuban Jam Session

Fania All Stars

Irakere

Kako, Totico y El Trabuco
La Máquina y El Motor

Kimbos, Los

Klimax

Libre, Conjunto

Lopez, Israel "Cachao"
Jam Session #2
Jam Session with Feeling

NG La Banda

Palmieri, Eddie

Papines, Los

Paulito y Su Elite

Puente, Tito
La Leyenda
Top Percussion
any other selections

Reve, Orquesta

Ritmo Oriental, Orquesta

Rojitas y su Orquesta

Son 14

Tipica 73

Valdés, Carlos "Patato"
Patato y Totico

Van Van, Los
Any albums, especially the work
recorded in 1974, with
Llegue, Llegue and Guararé
Ritmo y Candela (Round World Records)
"Afrocubanismo!" (Bembe 2012-2)

Buying these and other recordings:

Descarga Mail Order Catalogue
1 (800) 377-2647

Qbadisc
PO Box 1256
Old Chelsea Station
New York, NY 10011

Tower Records

Many other locations

OTHER GREAT TIMBALEROS TO LISTEN TO

Amat, José Eladio

Barreto, Guillermo

Conte, Luis

Delgado, Jimmy

Díaz, Daniel

Díaz, Ulpiano

Dueño, Endel

Egües, Blas

Formell, Samuel

Garcia, Richie

Irizarry, Ralph

Kako (Francisco Angelk Bastar)

Llovét, Yonder deJesus Peña

Marrero, Nicky

Nieto, Ubaldo

Oquendo, Manny

Puente, Tito

Revé, Elio

Sabater, Jimmy

Sánchez, Filiberto

Sánchez, José Manuel

Vilató, Orestes

Valdés, Amadito

Vizcaíno, Roberto

There are so many great timbaleros it is impossible to list them all. Thanks to all of you for your musical contributions.

GLOSSARY

abanico — literally, "fan"; a stylized roll played by the timbalero usually to signify a change in the music (i.e. from verse to chorus).

baqueteo — a style developed by Cuban tympanists, of playing beats on the shell or head while the fingers of the other hand "filled in."

bongo bell — also called cencerro, the bell played by the bongo player (bongocero) during certain sections of Afro-Cuban popular music styles.

campana — cowbell

cáscara — the shell of the timbales; the pattern played on the shell of the timbales.

chachachá — a Cuban music style, developed from the danzón, and created by Enrique Jorrín.

chacha bell — the bell, usually the smallest of the bells, played for chachachá and other styles.

charanga francesa and charanga — a Cuban musical group, developed in the early 20th century, which played danzón and danzonete, and later chachachá.

cinquillo cubano — a five note pattern derived from the Cuban contradanza.

clave — a five note pattern which serves as the foundation of many, if not all, styles of popular Afro-Cuban music.

comparsa (or conga de comparsa) — the specific musical group which plays the conga during carnival.

conga habanera — the Havana style of the cuban carnival rhythm, called conga.

conga oriental — the Santiago style of the cuban carnival rhythm, called conga.

contradanza — literally, the "country dance,"

this 18th century style of Cuban music was influenced by the European court and country dance.

danza — a 19th century musical and dance form which served as the precursor to the danzón.

danzón — a Cuban musical and dance form derived from the contradanza and danza.

ghosted notes — are notes which are played much more softly than a regular note.

guataca — hoe blade used in the conga de comparsa.

guayo — a larger version of the güiro.

güiro — a serrated gourd, scraped with a stick, very popular in Afro—Cuban, as well as other Latin American countries', music.

hembra — the female, in the case of this book, the larger of the two drums.

macho — the male, in the case of this book, the smaller of the two drums.

mambo — an up tempo Afro—Cuban popular music style, developed in the 40's and 50's.

mambo bell — the bell played by the timbalero in mambo style songs.

manoseo del cuero — a style of using hands and fingers developed by early Cuban tympanists.

marcha — literally "march," the name sometimes given to the conga part.

merensongo — an Afro-Cuban feel invented by Changuito.

montuno — the repeated syncopated vamp played by the piano.

mozambique — an Afro-Cuban rhythm invented by Pedro Izquierdo (Pello el Afrokán), at first used in the Cuban carnival, later popularized by Eddie Palmieri in New York.

orquesta típica — a Cuban musical group used to perform the contradanza.

pailas — a vessel of iron or copper used in the sugar cane factories of Cuba; another name given to timbales.

pailitas or pailitas cubanas — smaller in size then the paila, these instruments allowed the performed to sit while he played.

palitos — literally "sticks"; the sticks and pattern played during rumba.

pilón — a rhythm invented by Enrique Bonne in the eastern province of Cuba.

rumba — an Afro-Cuban folkloric musical form, consisting of drums, dance, and call and response. The three types of rumba are yambú, guaguancó, and columbia.

sobado — the name given to the sound played by the hand on the hembra, or low drum from the Spanish word "sobar"— to rub.
songo — a form of Cuban popular music which blends rumba, son, and other Afro-Cuban rhythms with jazz and funk.

timbalero — the timbale player.
timbales — a set of two, tuneable drums invented in Cuba. Timbales are the direct descendant of the European tympani.

timbalitos — smaller version of today's timbales.

timbalones — larger version of timbales, typically found in charangas.

timba songo layé — an Afro-Cuban feel invented by Changuito.

tumbadora — cubanized version of African drums, also referred to as the conga drum.

tumba francesa — a folkoric style developed in the Oriente (eastern) province of Cuba, developed by Africans who departed Haiti after the Haitian Revolution in 1791.

tumbao — the repeated pattern played by the tumbadoras or conga drums.